INTO THE

C000031203

RELIGIOUS EDUCATION IN

The Bible:
Literature &
Sacred Text

Benedict Hegarty OP

Series Editors
Eoin G. Cassidy and Patrick M. Devitt

VERITAS

First published 2003 by
Veritas Publications
7/8 Lower Abbey Street
Dublin 1
Ireland
Email publications@veritas.ie
Website www.veritas.ie

ISBN 1 85390 679 4

10 9 8 7 6 5 4 3 2 1

A catalogue record for this book is available from the British Library.

Cover design by Bill Bolger
Printed in the Republic of Ireland by Betaprint Ltd, Dublin

*Veritas books are printed on paper made from the wood pulp of managed
forests. For every tree felled, at least one tree is planted, thereby renewing
natural resources.*

Contents

Introduction   5

1   The Bible as Living Classic and Sacred Text   15

2   Text and Community   38

3   The Literature of the Bible   73

4   Biblical Texts   100

    Notes   122

Introduction

September 2003 saw the introduction of the Leaving Certificate Religious Education Syllabus by the Department of Education and Science. For those concerned to promote a religious sensibility in young Irish adults it is hard to exaggerate the importance of this event. It both represents a formal recognition by society of the value of religious education in the academic lives of second-level students, and it also reflects the importance which Irish society attaches to promoting the personal growth of students, including their spiritual and moral development. Religious education offers young people the opportunity to understand and interpret their experience in the light of a religious world-view. Furthermore, in and through an engagement with the RE Syllabus at Leaving Certificate level, students will learn a language that will enable them both to articulate their own faith experience and to dialogue with those of different faiths or non-theistic stances.

The Department of Education Syllabus is to be welcomed in that it gives recognition to the role that religious education plays in the human development of the young person. It is not an exaggeration to say that religious education is the capstone of the school's educational response to the young person's search for meaning and values. In this context, it encourages students to reflect upon their awareness of themselves as unique individuals with roots in a community network of family, friends and parish. Furthermore, it allows students to acknowledge and reflect upon their relationship to a God who cares for them and for the world in which we live. Finally, it gives students access to the universal nature of the quest for truth, beauty and goodness. Most of these themes are addressed sympathetically in the section entitled *The Search for Meaning and Values*. In particular, this section is to be welcomed because it offers the possibility for students to grapple with theistic and non-theistic world-views in a context that is hospitable to religious belief.

A critical dimension of the young person's educational journey is the growth in understanding of their own culture and the manner in which culture shapes their outlook on the world. The Religious Education Syllabus not only addresses the manner in which religion (and in particular Christianity) has shaped Irish culture over many centuries, but it also provides an extremely valuable platform from which to critique aspects of the relationship between faith and culture in the contemporary world. The section entitled *Religion: The Irish Experience* addresses the former concern by showing pupils the manner in which the Christian religion has contributed to the belief patterns and values of Irish society. It also alerts them to the depths of religious belief that predate by many centuries, even millennia, the arrival of Christianity in Ireland; and it also connects them to the cultural richness that links Ireland to the European continent. In this context, the devotional revolution that took place in Ireland (including the extraordinary growth in religious orders from 1850-1930) is a topic that could be expanded. The missionary outreach of the Catholic Church in Ireland in the last hundred years is worthy of special mention. Finally, students studying this section should be encouraged to acknowledge the ambiguities that have attended the presence of religion in Ireland over the centuries; to see on the one hand the image of an island of saints and scholars, and on the other hand to note how 'lilies that fester smell far worse than weeds'. In examining the manner in which faith and culture interact, the sections entitled *Religion and Science* and *Religion and Gender* make a valuable contribution to the Syllabus. These sections address topical issues that were controversial in the past and continue to be problematical even today. In treating of these two topics it is obviously important to avoid stereotypes – the acceptance of unexamined assumptions that mask or over-simply the truth to such an extent as to do a disservice to the seriousness of the issues involved. Likewise, the section on *World Religions* should be taught in a manner that is sensitive to the dangers of cultural and religious stereotypes. This section not only gives students a valuable introduction to the main religions in the world, but it also provides a cultural context for an awareness of the fact that the phenomenon of religion and the experience of religious belief is something that shapes people's understanding of themselves and their lifestyles across all cultural boundaries. Furthermore, it should never be forgotten that if, as Christians believe, God's Spirit is present in and through these religions, there is a need to study these religions precisely in order to discover aspects of God's presence in the world that has the capability to continually surprise.

In the Irish cultural context, Catholicism shapes the religious sensibilities and practices of the majority of young people. The Syllabus offers a generous acknowledgement of the importance of Christianity in the Irish context by providing two sections that focus on core aspects of the Christian faith. These are: *Christianity: origins and contemporary expressions* and *The Bible: Literature and Sacred text*. In this context, the Syllabus section on the Bible is to be welcomed. However, greater attention could be given to the role and significance of the Prophets in the Old Testament and to Paul in the New Testament. Furthermore, in studying the Bible it should never be forgotten that the primary reality is not the 'book' but rather the person of Christ and the community tradition grappling with this reality that is revealed in and through the Bible.

What is often in danger of being forgotten in an academic context is the importance of the fostering of attitudes and practices that promote personal growth. Religious education cannot be focused only on knowledge and understanding, because religion is primarily a way of celebrating life and, in particular, the spiritual dimension of life in and through the practices of worship, ritual and prayer. The Syllabus's recognition of this critical dimension of religious education through the section entitled *Worship, Ritual and Prayer* is to be welcomed. In addressing this section of the Syllabus it would be important to alert students to the great variety of spiritualities, prayer forms, mysticisms, rituals and styles of music that are to be found within the Christian tradition in order that students may have the possibility of exploring the richness of the spiritual dimension of their own tradition.

A key remit of the educational process is the fostering of moral maturity through a syllabus that allows students to engage in moral education. Not only is religious education particularly suited to facilitating this educational imperative, but the ethical character of human life is a core feature of all religions. The importance of this dimension of religious education is recognised in the provision of two sections entitled *Moral Decision Making* and *Issues of Justice and Peace*. There is nothing optional about the challenge to promote justice and peace. However, it is a topic that can all too easily be ideologically driven. Therefore, there is a special responsibility on those teaching this section to ensure that the instances of injustice cited, and the causes of injustice proposed, are grounded in solid research.

The challenges to Catholic religion teachers
Though religious education has been an integral part of Irish second-level schools long before the foundation of the state, it

has not until now been possible to assess this work under the State examination system. The reason for this anomaly is the Intermediate Education Act (1878) which allowed for the teaching but forbade the State examination of religious education. The removal of this legal constraint on State examination of RE has provided the impetus for the introduction of the Junior Certificate Syllabus in September 2000 and the introduction of the Leaving Certificate Syllabus in September 2003. These changes are to be welcomed but they provide a number of major challenges to Catholic religion teachers that should not be minimised.

In the *first* place, Catholic religion teachers have to attend to the danger that the new Syllabus will lead to a weakening of a commitment to catechesis in second level schools. The catechetical project of faith formation is built around six key pillars: knowledge of the faith; liturgical/sacramental education; moral formation; learning to pray; education for community life, including a fostering of the ecumenical character of Christian community, and finally, missionary initiative and inter-religious dialogue. Clearly, the RE Leaving Certificate Syllabus does give attention to many of the above themes, including the key catechetical concerns of attitude or value formation and the development of commitments. However, the emphasis in the Syllabus is undoubtedly upon the acquiring of knowledge, understanding and knowledge-based skills, all of which undoubtedly place it under the rubric of religious education rather than catechesis. The religion teacher ought to value the distinctive approaches to religion reflected in both catechesis and religious education. Both are important because both contribute in distinctive ways to the religious development of the young person. Catechesis aims at maturity of faith whereas religious education aims at knowledge and understanding of the faith.

From the point of view of the religion teacher, the teaching can have a different tone at different times. On one occasion, it might have a 'showing how' or catechetical tone, one that assumes a shared faith experience and encourages active participation. At another time it can have an educational or 'explaining' tone that invites pupils to stand back from religion to a certain extent, so that they can gain a more objective understanding of what is being taught. The Religious Education Syllabus should be taught in a manner that keeps both of these approaches in balance. In a similar vein, the presence of RE on the Leaving Certificate curriculum should not distract teachers from acknowledging that the religious development of young people happens in many contexts, which are distinct, though complementary. It can take place at home, in the parish, with friends as well as in school. Furthermore, even in the school it can take place at a whole series of levels including liturgy, prayer and projects that encourage an awareness of the need to care for those in most need.

In the *second* place, teachers have to attend to the scope and range of the aims of the Syllabus, one that seeks both to introduce students to a broad range of religious traditions and to the non-religious interpretation of life as well as providing students with the opportunity to develop an informed and critical understanding of the Christian tradition. In this context, teachers have to balance the need to promote tolerance for and mutual understanding of those of other or no religious traditions, alongside the need to give explicit attention to the Christian faith claims that Jesus is the Son of God and that he died to save us and to unite us with God and one another. Similarly, in teaching Christianity, teachers need to give attention to the role and significance of the Church from a Catholic perspective. It should never be forgotten that the idea of the Church as 'people of God', 'body of Christ' and 'temple of the Holy Spirit' is one that is at the heart of Catholic self-understanding.

In a similar vein, the Syllabus encourages students to engage critically with a wide variety of ethical codes with a view to the development of a moral maturity. Teachers will have to balance this approach with the way in which morality is viewed within the Christian tradition under the heading of discipleship – Jesus invites people to follow *him* rather than an ethical code or vision. Furthermore, from a Christian perspective, morality is never simply or even primarily concerned with a listing of moral prohibitions, rather it situates the ethical dimension of human nature within the context of a belief in a forgiving God. Finally, it should not be forgotten that it does not make sense to teach morality in too abstract a manner. Morality is something preeminently practical and at all times needs to be brought down to the level of real people – those who struggle with the demands of conscience in their lives. From a Catholic perspective, one has in the lives of the saints a multitude of examples of the manner in which people have attempted to follow the call to discipleship that is Christian morality.

Finally, nobody concerned with the seriousness of the challenge facing schools to promote moral maturity could be unaware of the importance of the contemporary challenge posed to the promotion of societal and religious values by the rise of a relativist and/or subjectivist ethos. In this context, the teaching of the broad variety of moral codes will have to be done in a manner that draws students' attention to the importance of acknowledging the objective nature of morality as opposed to accepting uncritically either a relativist or a subjectivist standpoint. In the light of the need to critique an exaggerated acceptance of pluralism, there is also a need to acknowledge that not all theories are equally valid, and moral decision-making is not simply a matter of applying one's own personal preference.

What is proposed in these commentaries
Given the breadth and scope of the Syllabus it is undoubtedly true that teachers will have to attend to the wide variety of sections in the Syllabus which demand a breadth of knowledge that some may find a little daunting. Even though it is not envisaged that teachers would attempt to teach all ten sections

of the Syllabus to any one group of students, nevertheless, the Syllabus will make demands upon teachers that can only be met if there are support services in place. For example, apart from the need to ensure the publishing of good quality teaching and learning resources, the schools themselves will need to ensure that appropriate resources – books, CDs, internet and videos – are provided. Finally, teachers will need to be provided with appropriate in-service training. It is to furthering this goal of providing good quality teaching and learning resources that the present series of volumes is addressed.

The eleven volumes in this series of commentaries comprise an introductory volume (already published, *Willingly To School*) that reflects upon the challenge of RE as an examination subject, along with ten other volumes that mirror the ten sections in the Syllabus. These commentaries on the Syllabus have been published to address the critical issue of the need to provide resources for the teaching of the Syllabus that are both academically rigorous and yet accessible to the educated general reader. Although primarily addressed to both specialist and general teachers of religion and third-level students studying to be religion teachers, the commentaries will be accessible to parents of Leaving Certificate pupils and, in addition, it is to be hoped that they will provide an important focus for adults in parish-based or other religious education or theology programmes. In the light of this focus, each of the volumes is structured in order to closely reflect the content of the Syllabus and its order of presentation. Furthermore, they are written in clear, easily accessible language and each includes an explanation of new theological and philosophical perspectives.

The volumes offered in this series are as follows

Patrick M. Devitt:	*Willingly to School: Religious Education as an Examination Subject*
Eoin G. Cassidy:	*The Search for Meaning and Values*
Thomas Norris and Brendan Leahy:	*Christianity: Origins and Contemporary Expressions*
Philip Barnes:	*World Religions*
Patrick Hannon:	*Moral Decision Making*
Sandra Cullen:	*Religion and Gender*
John Murray:	*Issues of Justice and Peace*
Christopher O'Donnell:	*Worship, Prayer and Ritual*
Benedict Hegarty:	*The Bible: Literature and Sacred Text*
John Walsh:	*Religion: The Irish Experience*
Fachtna McCarthy and Joseph McCann:	*Religion and Science*

Thanks are due to the generosity of our contributors who so readily agreed to write a commentary on each of the sections in the new Leaving Certificate Syllabus. Each of them brings to their commentary both academic expertise and a wealth of experience in the teaching of their particular area. In the light of this, one should not underestimate the contribution that they will make to the work of preparing teachers for this challenging project. Thanks are also due to our publishers, Veritas. Their unfailing encouragement and practical support has been of inestimable value to us and has ensured that these volumes saw the light of day. Finally, we hope that you the reader will find each of these commentaries helpful as you negotiate the paths of a new and challenging syllabus.

Eoin G. Cassidy
Patrick M. Devitt
Series Editors

I

The Bible as Living Classic and Sacred Text

1.1 THE BIBLE AS LIVING CLASSIC

Examples of classic texts taken from a variety of sources
Every year publishing houses churn out books, essays, poems in their thousands. Very few stand the test of time. Some are very much of their time, but do not appeal to later generations. A minority will appear again and again. They will be discussed, re-read, re-edited. Such books have that special quality which makes them a classic. They have a facility with language; they have the skill to explore the human condition in a new and gripping way. They have the ability to change the reader mysteriously and echo on in the mind long after the last page is read.

A classic is unsettling, questioning. It broadens the scope of our freedom and introduces us to a vista of possibilities of living. A classic opens up a range of connections and suggests a variety of interpretations. It can be read again and again with deep enjoyment. The classics are open-ended. They have an element of mystery that contains a surplus of meanings. Generation after generation can appropriate them in their own social and historical moment and allow them to unfold in a new setting. The classic survives because it has a perpetual modernity that enables it to live in successive layers of history and is never really perceived as ancient even when it is. In the words of Kermode: 'The books we call classics possess intrinsic qualities that endure, but possess also an openness to accommodation which keeps them alive under endlessly varying dispositions'.[1]

The strength of a classic can be seen in two examples, Emily Bronte's *Wuthering Heights* and Seamus Heaney's *Bogland*.

A novel such as *Wuthering Heights* can be read and re-read and there is always something new to be discovered, other possibilities of interpretation, new angles on the story. The rain-swept bleakness of the Yorkshire moors is immensely evocative. The characterisations are deep and full of resonance. The novel has an enigmatic quality that poses many questions as it explores passion, violent anger, evil, loss, death and the supernatural.

The dark brooding mulch of the bog is the physical image for Heaney's meditation on continuity with the past in his poem *Bogland*. The poem begins with a vivid contrast in scale, which itself is a reflection on American and Irish experiences. On one hand, there is the vastness of the prairie whose horizons were restlessly searched out by the wagon teams of the pioneers. The Irish image contracts to a lake that is the eye of the bog full of depth and mystery. The bog itself is the custodian of the past; it is its memory. The vegetable world is represented by the waterlogged trunks of the fir trees; the animal world by the empty skeleton of a Great Elk and human life by the buried butter. The whole thing is fluid; horizons melt into one another with levels of life reaching deep into the past.

The poem was published in 1969 when the 'troubles' in Northern Ireland began to heat up. The bog is a richly sensual image of the awareness of the nation remembering its long history. This history has depths and layers that shape the individual and national consciousness.

Testing the Bible as Classic

All the great religions have a central basic literature. The Old Testament fulfils that purpose for Jews and Christians. Islam has the Qur'an; Hinduism has its sacred literature, so has Buddhism and so on. The Book provides a sort of anchor and at the same time allows an enormous freedom of interpretation.

The Bible, however, is more than just a book. It is a classic. The Bible is one of the great classics of literature. In many ways it is a library of classics that have had a profound effect on civilisation. It fulfils the role of a classic. Read and re-read, it is the single most important influence on the imaginative tradition of Western literature, art and music, being a central source of inspiration and imagery. Frye writes: 'My interest in the subject began in my earliest days as a junior instructor, when I found myself teaching Milton and writing about Blake, two authors who were exceptionally Biblical even by the standards of English literature. I soon realised that a student of English literature who does not know the Bible does not understand a good deal of what is going on in what he reads'.[2]

For many centuries, literacy centred on being able to read the Bible. Some of the early translations standardised national languages. When Luther (1483–1546) published his translation, it unified the various German dialects and moulded the language. The King James Version had a profound impact on English. Some of the great classics of English literature draw their themes from the Bible. John Milton's (1608–74) greatest works, *Paradise Lost, Paradise Regained* and *Samson Agonistes* are based on the Bible. T.S. Eliot (1888–1965) wrote two famous poems around biblical themes, *Journey of the Magi*, and *A Song for Simeon*. Thomas Mann's epic *Joseph and his Brothers* was published in German from 1933 to 1944 and translated into English in 1949.

Manuscript production and illumination were lavished on the Bible. The Bible was the first book to be printed in Europe.

The visual arts, painting, sculpture, architecture, metal work, and stained glass have drawn on the Bible. Stained glass came into its own in the Gothic Cathedrals where it depicted generally biblical scenes. In the times of the Renaissance and Reformation, many of the great artists drew at least some of their subjects from the Bible, for example, Fra Angelico, Donatello, da Vinci, Dürer, Titian, Raphael.

Leonardo da Vinci's best known work is the *Last Supper* in the refectory of Santa Maria delle Grazie, Milan; Michelangelo's most famous work is the creation scene on the ceiling of the Sistine Chapel in Rome. Some of the most important work by contemporary Irish artists, such as Patrick Pye and others, have the same source for their material.

There is a profound sense that, in some way, the incarnation that is the visibility of God is prolonged by the artistic creation. The Bible has been the inspiration of musical works, hymns, masses, oratorios, motets, cantatas and contemporary rock music. Biblical texts are the content of much of the vocal music of Bach (1685–1750) and Handel (1685-1759). *St Matthew's Passion* by Bach uses the words of the Gospel account of the death of Jesus. Handel's *Messiah* is particularly well known; in it he uses texts from fourteen books of the Bible. Haydn (1732–1809) composed an oratorio on *The Creation*. Mendelssohn captures the fire and passion of the parts of the Second Book of Kings in *Elijah* and the words of Paul are breathed to life in his oratorio *St Paul*. In the modern scene, *Joseph and the Amazing Technicolor Dreamcoat*, *Godspell*, and *Jesus Christ Superstar* all drew their inspiration from the Bible.

The authors of the American Declaration of Independence were deeply aware of the biblical culture and mined a wide range of prophetical and New Testament teaching on the rights of the individual. When they penned the famous words 'all men are created equal' and 'they are endowed by their Creator with certain unalienable rights' the background text was Acts 10:34 'Truly I perceive that God shows no partiality'. See also

Rom 2:11; and Col 3:25. The 1948 United Nations Universal Declaration of Human Rights is in the same tradition. Article 1 has the words, 'All human beings are born free and equal in dignity and rights'.

The Bible has been a central source of inspiration and imagery because it questions life from so many viewpoints. The sprawling edifice of the Bible is best described as a book of books or a library that, coming from many different human situations, looks at us, speaks to us, teaches us. It does so by history, letter, sermon, analysis, proverb, truth grasped by the imagination in myth and story. The range is comprehensive.

- The historical books cast their material from a specific viewpoint. When the people obey God, their land prospers, when they disobey him there is disaster.
- In the Pentateuch, the law is given and also a vision of the spirit and meaning of law. There is no 'class legislation' – aristocrat and peasant are one. Rich and poor, free man and slave all receive a like punishment for a similar misdeed. There is a prevailing concern for the oppressed, the disinherited, the weak, the poor, and the afflicted with respect for human life and bodily integrity. There is no imprisonment, but the guilty party had to repay the damage by hard work, Ex. 21:22,32. The weak in society are the focus for special attention. The next of kin of a husband must marry his widow to prevent her losing her home and security, Deut 25:5-10. The alien is protected, Lev 19:34; Deut 16:12. When the time comes for a slave to be liberated he must be set up in business, Deut 15:12-15.
- The personal touch and sense of involvement is found everywhere in the letters of St Paul. 'Timothy, who is working with me, sends his greetings ... I Tertius, who wrote out this letter, greet you in the Lord', Rom 16. 'All the churches of Asia send you greetings. Aquila and Prisca send you their warmest wishes ... This greeting is in my own hand', 1 Cor 16. 'Take

good note of what I am adding in my own handwriting and in large letters', Gal 6:11. 'Please give my greetings to the brothers at Laodicea and to Nympha and the church which meets in her house ... Here is a greeting in my own handwriting', Col 4:15-18. 'From me, Paul, these greetings in my own handwriting, which is the mark of genuineness in every letter; this is my own writing', 2 Thes 3:17.

- Pastoral peace is found in the psalms. 'The Lord is my shepherd there is nothing I shall want. Fresh and green are the pastures where he gives me repose. Near restful waters he leads me to revive my drooping spirit.' Ps 23:1-3.

- In vivid language the prophets rage against the society of their day. Amos condemns social injustice with ruthless severity. He describes the wealthy merchants with their lust for economic power as they trample on the heads of the poor and defenceless. '... they have sold the virtuous man for silver and the poor man for a pair of sandals, because they trample on the heads of ordinary people and push the poor out of their path', Amos 2:6-7. The public leaders revel in luxury and are corrupted by indulgence, unconcerned over the ruin of their country. He compares the society ladies to the fat, sleek cows of Bashan selfishly urging their husbands to injustice for drunken excess. 'Listen to this word, you cows of Bashan living on the mountain of Samara oppressing the needy, crushing the poor, saying to your husbands "Bring us something to drink!"', Amos 4:1. Like many a prophet, he deals devastating attacks on hypocritical religious practice. 'I hate and despise your feasts, I take no pleasure in your solemn festivals ... Let me have no more of the din of your chanting, no more of your strumming on harps. But let justice flow like water, and integrity like an unfailing stream', Amos 5:21-4.

- Some of the Biblical material is richly reflective. 'Yes, naturally stupid are all men who have not known God and who, from the good things that are seen, have not been able to discover Him-who-is or, by studying the works, have failed to recognise the Artificer. Fire however, or wind, or the swift air, the sphere of the stars, impetuous water, heaven's lamps, are what they have held to be the gods who govern the world. If, charmed by their beauty, they have taken things for gods, let them know how much the Lord of these excels them, since the very Author of beauty has created them. And if they have been impressed by their power and energy let them deduce from these how much mightier is he that has formed them, since through the grandeur and beauty of the creatures we may, by analogy, contemplate their Author', Wis 13:1-5.

- There is sober wisdom in the advice of 'Be steady in your conviction, sincere in your speech. Be quick to listen and deliberate in giving an answer. If you understand the matter, give your neighbour an answer, if not, put your hand over your mouth', Ecc 5:10-14.
- The haunting cadences of Ecclesiastes give a sense of the futility of life. 'Vanity of vanities, Qoheleth says. Vanity of vanities. All is vanity!', Ecc 1:2.
- The Song of Songs with its playful sensuousness is a delight. 'I hear my Beloved. See how he comes leaping on the mountains bounding over the hills. My beloved is like a gazelle, like a young stag. My Beloved lifts up his voice. He says to me, "come then, my love, my lovely one, come. For see, winter is past, rains are over and gone. The flowers appear on the earth. The season of glad songs has come, the cooing of the turtledove is heard in our land."' Song 2:10-12.
- The story of Jesus with its sharply crafted sayings, its challenging vision and ultimately triumphant love has captivated people through the ages.

The Influence of the Language of the Bible
The biblical message of care for the neighbour has reverberated down through the centuries. In the coldness of pagan society,

the early Christian communities were places of warmth and support. Following the teachings of Christ, the great monasteries were the only places of medical care for centuries. State involvement in health care and education is a modern occurrence. Until then, religious orders and congregations met the biblical challenge of service. For centuries, the Churches ran the schools and hospitals.

In South America, from the beginnings of colonial expansion, the Gospel values of justice, liberty, peace and reconciliation motivated many evangelists and missionaries. People such as Bartolomé de Las Casas (1484–1566), Antonio de Montesinos, Antonio Vieira (1608–1697) vigorously protested against the treatment of the indigenous peoples and the rural and urban poor. The words of a sermon by Antonio de Montesinos preached in 1511 are powerful and eloquent. 'I have come up on this pulpit, I who am a voice of Christ crying in the wilderness of this island. This voice says that you are in mortal sin … for the cruelty and tyranny you use in dealing with these innocent people. Tell me, by what right or justice do you keep these Indians in such cruel and horrible servitude?' Bartolomé de Las Casas is equally eloquent. 'What we committed in the Indies stands out among the most unpardonable offences ever committed against God and mankind and this trade [in Indian slaves] as one of the most unjust, evil, and cruel among them.'

In modern times, Archbishop Oscar Romero spoke up for the tortured, the slaughtered and the 'disappeared' of El Salvador. He was shot dead while saying Mass. In the sermon just minutes before his death, he spoke in the words of Jesus telling the story of the wheat, Jn 12:24. 'Those who surrender to the service of the poor through love of Christ, will live like the grain of wheat that dies. It only apparently dies. If it were not to die, it would remain a solitary grain. The harvest comes because of the grain that dies. We know that every effort to improve society, above all when society is so full of injustice and sin, is an effort that God blesses; that God wants; that God demands of us.'

Today, in the sprawling urban shanty towns, groups of people find new hope, dignity and a sense of justice as they pray with the Bible. Linking the Gospel to issues of poverty, justice, social and political liberation has given rise to liberation theology. This is an attempt to give a systematic Christian understanding based on the Bible to the people's dreams and struggles for a better life.

1.2   THE BIBLE AS SACRED TEXT

The Bible as revelation

Individuals and societies have various ways of coping with life. For some the ideal situation is total control of one's circumstances. In this view, happiness is determined by achievement, success and payoffs. Others would dream of escaping the dreariness and competitiveness of life to live in perfect love or a rustic idyll as respectable dropouts. Real life, however, has to cope with failure, boredom, sickness, and struggle. Real life has to take on board the dark times as well as the light-filled ones. It is living in time with memories, visions, love and struggle, grief and death.

Because of its historical context, the Biblical vision focuses in on real life and on God as a partner within it. Revelation is not the disclosure of abstract, timeless doctrines. It is about encountering a faithful, just and gracious God in the give and take of history. It is about concrete situations. It is about people living in community experiencing cost and joy. It is about hope for a society in which the starving will be fed, Lk 1:53, in which the last will be first, Lk 13:30 and the downtrodden will be lifted up and those in tears will be comforted, Mt 5:4. This is all not a dream, but a practical task to be accomplished in the ambiguities and chances of history. It teaches that the possibilities of this vision are breaking in now and are the task of every individual. In the Bible, God reveals himself and his ways in practical situations and thus shows alternative and betters ways of living life.

The Revealing Word of God

Words are symbols that facilitate the touching of minds. They are designed to help people disclose themselves to one another. A written word is just a scratching on a page until an eye looks at it; a spoken word is only a vibration in the air until an ear receives it. A word is an event that does not exist outside the context of communication.

We link the Word of God and revelation. Revelation tells us something of God; it gives us information. However, it would be a mistake to link it solely with ideas or the informational statements of the Creeds.

In our day-to-day communication with each other, we reveal far more than factual information – our age, our background, our job. We also reveal something of the quality of our presence, our warmth or lack of it; our patience or impatience; our straightforwardness or our shiftiness; our fidelity or unreliability; our love or hate. Communication goes far beyond ideas. Likewise, the Word of God is the context of a living engagement between God and us that involves information and the revelation of presence, loving kindness, promise and purpose on one side, and a loving faith and surrender on the other.

God is described as creating everything by speaking, Gen 1:1-2:3. The implication is that all that exists is a word of God. And so the psalmist can proclaim, 'The heavens are telling the glory of God; and the firmament proclaims his handiwork... their voice goes out through all the earth, and their words to the end of the world.' Ps 19:1-4.

Nevertheless, according to Jewish and Christian tradition the Bible has a special character. The Book is the Book of God:

the Word of God. It is described as inspired by God and is seen as the privileged context of his revealing word.

This conviction is seen in the reverence that the Jews, including Jesus and the disciples, had for the Law, the prophets and the writings. The Epistle to the Hebrews describes a biblical text as a word from God. 'To which of the angels did God ever say "You are my Son; today I have begotten you"', Heb 1:5. The author was quoting from Psalm 2:7. In the Second Letter to Timothy it is clearly said, 'All scripture is inspired by God and is useful for teaching, for reproof, for correction, for training in righteousness', 2 Tim 3:16.

Taking up this theme the patristic and medieval believers were content to affirm the divine authority of the books without probing too much into what shape that authority takes. The authors were described as the harps, lyres or flutes of the Holy Spirit caught or held by his influence. The letters were writings addressed by God to his faithful. They had little to say about the human author and their main emphasis was on the divine action.

This line of thinking was continued into the nineteenth century when the scholarly disciplines used in secular academic research were now applied to the Bible. The Biblical texts were analysed the same way as any other ancient text. Styles were compared. The historical truth of details was questioned. Critical studies discovered mistakes, contradictions and unevenness in the text. The academics seemed more interested in demolishing the Word of God than in preserving or expounding it. Charles Darwin and his theories of evolution were seen to severely undermine the Adam and Eve story. When the archaeologists discovered literary texts in the ruins of ancient cities it appeared that the story of Noah was an epic borrowed from the folklore literature of the ancient Near East. Questions arose about the New Testament. Who wrote the Gospels? If they do not come immediately from the eyewitness of the apostolic authors, what historical and religious authority can they have?

It became abundantly clear that the Bible had very human authors. How then could it claim a divine authorship as well? What form could the divine authorship take?

Reading in Context

The Bible must be seen as it is. The Bible is not a carefully produced piece of literature in which each part harmonises with the next. It is an interlocking collection of texts in which many elements are in tension with others. A brick does not make a house and neither does an individual text make the Word of God. It must be read in its environment and its environment reveals a gradual evolution of insight over a thousand years and more coupled with a variety of approaches and attitudes. This development had not gone smoothly. Cul-de-sacs were explored and rejected; wrong emphases taught and tempered. And so the command to utterly wipe out one's enemies and their families in some parts of the Old Testament, Deut 7:2; 20:16-17: Jos 6:17-18; 1 Sam 15:3, must be read against Jesus' words about loving your enemies; the community that produced the Fourth Gospel seems to be inward looking and self-absorbed in its orientation, but this is balanced by the exuberant missionary zeal of St Paul.

At the centre of the entire literary process is the living Word of God who is Jesus Christ. The Bible exists to give us the mental and emotional machinery to help us understand him. The Old Testament has its flashes of idealism, cynicism, moments of hope and despair, passages on the drudgery of human living, sinfulness, joy, question and doubt; human life in all its various forms is reflected there. All this gives a backdrop, a controlled environment for the Word to appear and be seen in the light of all the searching, losses and hopes. Likewise, the New Testament authors remembered and wrote as best they could. So too their role comes from their closeness to the Word made flesh.

The Living Word of God is the context in which the written text is to be understood. He is complete while each individual text only gives a flash of insight into him. All the individual texts must be gathered together in the light of Christ.

No one text of the Bible can be taken in isolation from the rest of the Bible. So each text is to be seen in a series of larger contexts.

Furthermore, the Book of the Bible itself must be read in that community which lives around Christ and learns from the experience of Him, each other, the living momentum of the past and the challenges of the future. It is the foundational text of the Christian community. Like the constitution of any nation, it is not a musty relic passed on from the past. Every nation has a process that interprets and applies its basic laws in new situations. So too, the Christian community in its liturgy, reflection, teachings draws out the meaning of the written Word of God for each generation.

Inspiration

It is the constant teaching of the Christian faith that the Holy Spirit was involved in the composition of the Bible. In practice, how did this work out?

It seems clear that under normal circumstances the biblical authors would be unaware of any special push or influence of the Spirit. They worked away as best they could using their own powers and energies. Yet they fitted into a master plan of God. He pushed, nudged them. The Holy Spirit is at work in the whole of the People of God of the Old and New Testaments building it up, inspiring, calling and challenging. In that general context, the Holy Spirit is at work in the production of the Book – but in a sophisticated way – adapted to peoples' knowledge, guaranteeing the general direction of their religious quest, suggesting deep in the author's psyche that he should write; illuminating his judgement as to what themes, details or events he would write down. This spirit is operative in the whole process which led to the composition of the piece of literature, the formation of the tradition, drafts, redrafts until the final text.

He is at work in the production of these books, but with a specific providence and direction. This particular task and its outcome are to provide a specific sort of literature which will be the constitution of the people of God. Their work became part of a total collection of books that together were the written account of God's revelation and his call to life.

The delicate interplay between divine and human action is described in *The Constitution of Divine Revelation*, chapter 3 from the Second Vatican Council. 'The divinely revealed realities, which are contained and presented in the text of sacred Scripture, have been written down under the inspiration of the Holy Spirit. For Holy Mother Church relying on the faith of the apostolic age, accepts as sacred and canonical the books of the Old and the New Testaments, whole and entire, with all their parts, on the grounds, that, written under the inspiration of the Holy Spirit (cf. Jn 20:31; 2 Tim 3:16; 2 Pet 1:19-21; 3:15-16), they have God as their author, and have been handed on as such to the Church herself. To compose the sacred books, God chose certain men who, all the while he employed them in this task, made full use of their powers and faculties so that, though he acted in them and by them, it was as true authors that they consigned to writing whatever he wanted written, and no more', # 11.[3]

If the Bible is God's word, it must be true. What's the truth of this literature? Galileo, like Copernicus, was convinced that the earth was not the centre of the universe, but that it revolved around the sun. This appeared to contradict certain biblical texts (for a more thorough exploration of this topic, see the commentary on Religion and Science). Galileo in 1633 was forced to recant on his views and condemned to imprisonment as 'vehemently suspected of heresy'. There was the famous case in 1925 of the State of Tennessee against John Scopes. The biblical text gives only a very special insight into God's Word, namely, in its significance for the ultimate goals of human life. This gave rise to many difficulties over the years. However, with the new insights into the world we live in, the form of truth involved was gradually seen. The Bible teaches truly that truth that is relevant to one's salvation. Since, therefore, all that the inspired authors, or sacred writers, affirm should be regarded as affirmed by the Holy Spirit, we must acknowledge that the books of Scripture firmly, faithfully and without error, teach that truth which God, for the sake of our salvation, wished to see confided to the sacred Scriptures. Thus 'all Scripture is inspired by God, and profitable for teaching, for reproof, for correction and for training in righteousness, so that the man of God may be complete, equipped for every good work' (2 Tim 3:16-17, Gk. text)'[4]. The Bible is about theology and not astronomy, the origin of the species or geology. At every level of its composition, the intention of a biblical text is to recall the community to faith and help it understand itself and its mission under God in particular circumstances. In the pursuit of that objective popular knowledge was used, traditions and myths were employed, history was retold. It does not matter if the popular science of three thousand years ago does not fit in with what we know; that is not the point of the biblical writing. When the biblical authors mulled over their history and narrated its events, they were calling their contemporaries to renew their faith in a God ever present to his people. Over a span of more than a thousand years, the Bible witnesses to the presence of God in the life of his people calling them to cope with the ever changing landscape of time and experience and to use their traditions and faith to forge new meanings in new situations in ways that are in continuity with the past. The truth of the Bible is found in the larger picture of God's presence, promises and demands and what these mean for the community of faith.

The formation and understandings of the canon

The word 'canon' is from the Greek 'kanon' meaning rule. The Bible is seen as the text that rules the Christian life. As a written text, it is an unchanging point of reference in all the centrifugal forces of culture and history in the millennia of Jewish and Christian belief. Scripture is often called 'The Rule of Faith'.

In the formative period of the People of God of the Old and New Testaments the process of selecting books to form the canon was underway. The task of selecting and ordering the books written in the Hebrew language was probably begun in the early fourth century BCE, and it was completed only in about 70 CE. It was then that the guiding list, the 'canon' of the Hebrew language scriptures of the Old Testament was fixed.

Before this, however, Jewish scholars in Egypt had translated many of these Hebrew books into Greek. They called this translation the Septuagint and it was nearly completed at the end of the second century BCE. Its list of authoritative scriptures is larger than the Hebrew canon. It also contains those books which are called the deutero-canonical books – Judith, Tobit, Sirach, Baruch, 1 and 2 Maccabees and the Wisdom of Solomon.

The Christian canon of the books of the Old and New Testaments was assembled over a long period of time. Opinions on its content differed from place to place and sometimes indeed in the same place at different times. 'The canon, in short, was only finally determined on the basis of long experience of the Church with a large variety of writings, some of which, in that collective experience, were to be included in the canon, and hence to be regarded as authoritatively inspired, while others were to be excluded, and hence to be regarded as lacking in such inspiration'.[5]

There were various stimuli contributing to the establishment of the canon. One such was the attempt by Marcion in the second century, to form his own canon. Marcion came to Rome around the year 140 CE. Because he believed that the God of the Old Testament was evil, he rejected the whole of the Old Testament, the Gospels of Matthew, Mark and John and was left with the epistles of St Paul with favourable references to the Law cut out plus an edited version of the

Gospel of St Luke. There were further difficulties with other groups that claimed the Holy Spirit spoke through them in the same way that he spoke through the original disciples. All this made it urgent for the Church to make up its mind as to what was canonical or not and the establishment of a defined group of books which would be collectively normative.

The synods of Hippo (393) and Carthage (397) are important milestones in the final establishment of the Canon. It is not that these councils fixed the canon, the Christian communities, whose experience determined which books were useful and which were not, fixed the canon. Underpinning the tortuous human process was the activity of the Holy Spirit that guided the forces that produced the Bible in the first place and guided the community to recognise itself and God's hand in a definite select and exclusive collection of book.

There were other books in circulation in the early Church that were not included in the canon. Two of these would be the Gospel of Thomas and the Acts of Paul and Thecla. The Epistle of Barnabas was highly esteemed in the early Church. It was written around the year 130 CE and interprets the rites, ceremonies and laws of the Old Testament as pointers to Christ. In some circles it was accepted as canonical only to be firmly rejected later on.

Biblical interpretation today

The Bible is not a book whose meaning is immediately obvious. It was written by people from a different culture to ours, with different information, interests and languages. The Bible needs to be worked by various levels of scholarship so that we can reconstruct the world from which it came and understand it better as a social document and a multifaceted collection of literatures.

Biblical criticism

The scientific study of the Bible is normally called 'criticism'. Now that word can create the wrong impression. Criticism can

seem negative, denigratory, carping. When applied to the Bible
it can seem as an attempt to destroy its authority and
undermine its role at the heart of the Christian faith. However,
the word can have a much more positive meaning. When we
talk about music criticism, we are not attacking music as such.
A music critic attempts to describe the best interpretation of a
piece of music, draw out its qualities and promote standards.

It is in this latter sense that we speak of Biblical criticism. It
is the attempt to understand the Bible in the light of the best
investigative standards and all available information.

The Bible is a collection of literature written a long time ago
and over a long age span and as such a number of basic
questions have to be asked if we are to understand it properly.

Textual Criticism
The first and obvious one is: do we have the right text. A
distance of nineteen hundred years separates us from the first
appearance of the last book of the Bible. How did it fare in the
intervening centuries? If the original words are the authentic
version, how can we be sure that our one is accurate and
corresponds to the original text? For centuries the Bible was
laboriously copied out by hand. Sometimes the scribe had a
version on his desk that he read and followed, other times it was
dictated and several scribes would make their copies
simultaneously. In the copying and transmission of manuscripts
mistakes – deliberate and unintentional – can happen. A word
can be misread or misheard. Simple fatigue can lead to
confused words, omissions. To clear up difficulties, scribes can
emend the text to what they think is the right version, but they
can be wrong. To solve these various problems, the textual
critic tries to correct the manuscript to the version that was first
composed by the author.

It is not as if the critic is short of manuscripts to work on.
From the early centuries of Christianity there are some five
thousand Greek manuscripts that contain either the whole or

part of the New Testament. The original Greek text can be inferred from the very early translations made into Latin, Coptic, Syriac, Armenian, Gothic, Ethiopic and Old Slavonic.

Towards the end of the first century CE Jewish scholars settled on an agreed text of the Hebrew Bible. This is called the Massoretic text. This was preserved carefully over the centuries. In caves in the desert by the Dead Sea, Hebrew manuscripts of the Old Testament were discovered in 1948. These are called the Dead Sea Scrolls and are dated from the first century. It was found that there was very little difference between the Hebrew text then and the Massoretic text that is printed in modern Hebrew language Old Testaments.

A textual critic makes a decision on the authentic text using his experience, his knowledge of the history of the manuscripts he is dealing with, and applying common sense. Some working principles are often mentioned, one of which is that the more difficult reading is preferable. The instinct of the scribe was to make a difficult text more understandable than vice-versa.

Linguistics

The next issue is that of language. We use translations. Can we be confident that these translations convey the true meaning of the text? Linguistics is involved in the study of the languages used in the Bible. These are Hebrew and Greek with a little Aramaic. The linguist studies the exact meaning of the words in their own time and place.

Literary Criticism

Having established the text and the meaning of the words, the next layer of analysis is called literary criticism: a written document can take many forms and must be interpreted according to its individual nature.

History, story, myth all have their own truth, but they cannot be confused with one another. If a story is read as history or a myth understood to be scientific fact, they are being measured by standards that are not of their own nature. The literary critic has to find out if an individual text or book is history, poetry, a legal code or a collection of proverbs. A classic example would be the opening chapters of the Book of Genesis. What is on the agenda of these chapters? Are they about science? If so, they are in serious conflict with contemporary theories on the origin of the universe and the evolution of the species. Or are they largely mythological? Here again we run into problems. The mythological is often unfavourably contrasted with the historical or scientific. The critic analyses the role of the Genesis myths and shows that they are dealing with truth, but in their own way. Genesis is not really about talkative serpents, species of apples, a woman made from a rib, or light created before either the sun or the moon. It is about various issues including the roots of evil in human choice, the equality of the sexes, and the blessings of creation. Other questions can arise about a Biblical text. For instance, is it one document or two? An example would be the Book of Isaiah. It is shown to be a compilation of three clearly distinct documents that were written over a period of three hundred years and reflect very different historical circumstances. Another book could have gone through various stages in its composition. Anomalies in the Gospel of St John are best explained by various editions of the work in which additional material was added without the editorial pruning that would bridge the seams between the old and the new. A critic asks, what are the sources of the material? A classic example of this would be the synoptic problem and the dependency relationship of the first three Gospels on one another. When the ancient Egypt document, the Sayings of Amenemopet, was discovered in 1922 it became clear that the Book of Proverbs used it as a source for several chapters. Within the Pentateuch, the first five books of the Bible, it is possible to distinguish various sources or traditions that were interwoven in the text. How does a particular passage fit into its context? An associated issue would be the identification of the authorship of the individual books if that were possible.

Historical criticism examines the history that the Biblical text relates. Is there independent confirmation of events, peoples and life-styles that are mentioned in the Bible. Is the Biblical witness to history coherent in itself? Using other sources, can the Biblical history be set in a wider context?

Archaeology is very relevant here. Until the nineteenth century, the Bible was almost the sole source of information about the times and peoples that are mentioned in its text. This was particularly so of Old Testament times. This has changed dramatically. The science of archaeology has thrown a flood of light on the civilisations of which the biblical world was a tiny part. It does so through the excavation and study of the remains of ancient towns, buildings and artefacts.

Tens of thousands of written sources have been unearthed from the past. These are mostly texts written on clay and baked to preserve them. These can be commercial records, religious texts, and diplomatic and military despatches. They were stored in the archives of ancient cities in Syria, Egypt and Mesopotamia. Some of the texts were written on papyrus. This was particularly so of Egyptian records. Papyrus is a type of paper made by gluing together the reeds of the papyrus plant. These documents cast light on the world in which the biblical people lived. The records have also given details of cities and civilisations that previously were practically unknown. The Dead Sea Scrolls are one of the most famous collections of documents to be discovered. These were found in a series of sites close to the Dead Sea from 1947 to 1960. Many of the scrolls are copies of biblical books. There are also a number of non-biblical religious texts. The monastery that produced the documents was excavated subsequent to the discovery of the Scrolls

Apart from the Scrolls, not many documents have been found in Palestine itself. What has been discovered is a wealth of detail on the day-to-day lives of people over an extended period of time. This would include the shape and size of cities; their fortifications, public buildings and private homes. A comprehensive picture of ancient life can be formed. How they lived, what they ate, status in society, their relationship with the surrounding world, and trading contacts can be established by the particular styles and types of artefacts spread over a period. Using his skill, knowledge and imagination the archaeologist digs up people.

Excavations in the Church or the Holy Sepulchre in Jerusalem have confirmed the tradition that it is the place of the Crucifixion and burial of Christ. Archaeologists can now give a more detailed picture of the Jerusalem Temple that was the scene of memorable moments in the life of Jesus. Perhaps the most evocative excavation is the one in Capernaum. Jesus lived in Capernaum, Mk 2:1, for a while and preached in the synagogue, Mk 1:21-28. The excavators unearthed two octagonal walls one inside the other. These were built on some older structures of much ruder construction and are now visible. These are the remains of fishermen's houses from the first century CE. Inscriptions scratched on the plastered walls of one of these huts reveal that it was a place where Christians gathered. The octagonal walls are the remains of a Christian church that was built on the site in the third century. Clearly Christians revered this little group of houses at a very early stage in the history of the Church. It is a reasonable inference that they believed that here was the house of Peter where Jesus lodged, Mt 8:20. The remains of the synagogue in which Jesus preached has also been uncovered.

Redaction Criticism
This is an attempt to understand the mindset of the individual author of a biblical book. What motivates him? What does he

think is important? The raw material of the Gospels is the tradition of sayings and stories about Christ. Out of this the evangelists composed quite different Gospels. They did so out of a specific theology that led them to select some material, reject others, combine texts in different orders, shape or prune the material. Redaction criticism attempts to map the shape of this framework. The way the story is told tells us something about the author. This is particularly evident in the historical books of the Bible. The facts and figures of biblical history are selected and presented to fit into a particular theological programme.

Reflecting on biblical criticism in general, the American scholar Bernard Anderson writes, 'Modern biblical criticism has helped us to understand the humanity of the Word of God in the Bible. It has taught us that Scripture is historically conditioned: its words are the words of human beings who lived in particular times, who acted and thought in the sociological context of their society, who were immersed in the wider culture of the ancient Near East. It has taught us that Scripture is not a monolithic whole but, rather, presents a wonderful wealth of human diversity and theological pluralism. It has taught us that much of what is related in Scripture should not be regarded as straightforward history, in the modern sense, but must be regarded as legend, saga, and poetry.'[6]

2

Text and Community

2.1 THE FORMATION OF THE HEBREW SCRIPTURES

Oral tradition

Even today, in families and localities a substantial amount of information is passed on by word of mouth. Anecdotes are shared about parents and grandparents. Fields and hills and laneways have their story. 'The whole landscape a manuscript', wrote the Irish poet, John Montague.

'In the beginning was the Word'. That is the context in which the Biblical tradition first saw the light of day. 'Hear, Israel', Deut 6:4, starts the instruction which each Jewish believer had to recite daily. The bulk of biblical material was first presented as word of mouth before being written down. That was the normal method of communication in the ancient world. Peoples' memories were better. They did not rely on the written text. A community would pass on its traditions, epics, laws told around the fire at night, while gathered for worship or celebration. The sayings of the wise would be memorised and passed on.

Israelite literature started around the reign of David. Before that, the stories, epics and myths of the people were passed on orally. Much of the prophetic literature was first composed for oral delivery and transmission. The same could be said of large amounts of the historical tradition.

The preservation of the tradition and the formation of the community

In this form of transmission the role of the community is crucial. The words of the spokesman will only be accepted if in some way they reflect what the community regards as true and gives voice to its values and historical self-understanding. A creativity is allowed to the declaimer as long as he stays within familiar perimeters. This is the case even when the speaker, like one of the prophets, is critical of the community. In the telling of the stories, the group reclaims its memories, and in the process, strengthens its sense of cohesion. The sense of group identity therefore has a control over the material that it never would over a written text.

Some of these traditions would have belonged to an individual tribe. Others would have been part of the liturgy of specific sanctuaries. The great prophets had schools of followers who memorised their sayings. The elders and judges of the Israelite towns and villages preserved and developed the covenant legal traditions.

The political unity achieved by David led to collection of the various traditions into a normative piece of literature for all the tribes. Once this process was started, the literature expanded until the final texts of the Old Testament were written down.

Even as a piece of literature, the oral antecedents of the text were never forgotten. When the law was written by the priests and scribes, it still had to be proclaimed aloud to the people of God. That is why in 622 BCE the king, Josiah 'read in their hearing all the words of the book of the covenant', 2 Kgs:23.2 and some hundreds of years later, Ezra did the same, Neh 8.1-8. The deacon Philip heard the Ethiopian reading from the scroll of Isaiah, Acts 8:28,30. Other sections of the Biblical text were first intended to be sung. That was the way with most of the psalms, the songs of Miriam and Deborah, Ex 15:21; and Judg 5. The intended process is well described in a New Testament text, 'Blessed is the one who reads aloud the words of the prophecy, and blessed are those who hear and who keep what is written in it', Rev 1:3. It is a living process from mouth to heart. 'Faith comes from what is heard, and what is heard comes through the word of Christ', Rom 10:17.

In the first century CE, the rabbis, the Jewish teachers, entrusted their teachings to living minds to be memorised and transmitted by word of mouth. This was so even when ample literary resources were available to them. The written text was mediated, expounded, developed by word of mouth. All this rests on a fundamental insight. The Word of God is not the dead letter of a text, but living communication mediated by God's Spirit, human prayer, struggle and experience. This means that the Word is reactivated for each generation in a living experience.

The development of writing

Writing or a form of writing is found in most advanced ancient civilisations. It seems to have been first invented in Mesopotamia sometime before about 3100 BCE. Soon afterwards it appeared in Egypt. Population growth in the valleys of the Nile and the Euphrates encouraged more complex social and economic organisation. Trade links grew as surplus production became possible through irrigation and land reclamation. There was the need to mark one's goods clearly and therefore seals were invented to fulfil that purpose. The supply of goods from one to another demanded a tally kept by both parties. At first such records were simple enough. The earliest writings consisted of pictures depicting the trade goods with strokes and notches to indicate the numbers involved. Pictures were then used to depict abstract words that sounded the same or sounded like the syllables in a larger word. This led to syllabic writing. Consonants and vowels were not separated from one another and therefore granted the multitude of syllables in any language the number of signs to write them is very large. The total number was evened out at about six hundred.

There are two types of syllabic writings, cuneiform and hieroglyphic. The word 'cuneiform' is from the Latin *cuneus* meaning wedge. The symbols in their advanced form looked like wedges and were made by strokes imprinted on wet clay by a pointed stylus. This was held at an angle and the tapered point pressed into the clay left a wedge-shaped mark. The hieroglyphs, named from the Greek 'sacred scratchings' were more obviously a form of picture writing than cuneiform. Hieroglyphic writing is associated with Egypt. Sometime around the year 2000 BCE, a genius living between Asia Minor and Egypt isolated the consonants from the vowels and used signs for the consonants only. This simplified enormously the whole system. It reduced the number of signs from hundreds to some twenty or thirty. When the Greeks borrowed this system in the eighth Century BCE, they discovered that there were signs which had nothing corresponding to them in Greek and these surplus signs were used to designate the vowels. This new system took over across the world except in China and Japan where the older pictographic script is still in use.

The three phases of the historical narratives – The Torah, the Deuteronomic Literature, and the Chronicler's History
There are three blocks of historical narrative in the Old Testament. Each block is made up of individual books, but they can be grouped according to characteristic interests that they share.

The Torah
The word 'torah' is normally translated as 'law' and the books gathered under this title are also called the Pentateuch, the first five books of the Bible. The importance of the Torah for the

understanding of Biblical history lies less in the factual details and more in the vision of history itself that underpins it.

The historical narrative begins with the migration of Abraham and other family members from Ur in Mesopotamia to Haran. The third Dynasty of Ur was destroyed towards the end of the twentieth century by groups of peoples. These were the Elamites, who moved in from the East, and the Amorites, a nomadic people who infiltrated from the steppes to the west. It is possible that Abraham's family belonged to one of these Amorite groups who settled in Ur at that time and later departed from the disturbed and declining city of Ur to the more prosperous Haran in the north.

The account continues with the call of Abraham in Genesis 12 followed by various descents to Egypt. There are many Egyptian records that refer to the arrival of Semites in Egypt as traders, in times of famine or as captives. An early nineteenth-century wall painting comes from Beni-Hasan, 169 miles above Cairo. It is from a tomb and shows a group of thirty-seven desert dwellers bringing gifts and looking for trade. Eventually these people who gradually infiltrated Egypt took over and by the middle of the second millennium ruled the land and were called Hyksos.

With the re-emergence of Egyptian nationalism and the expulsion of the Hyksos, it could well be that the remnants of the Hyksos, other captives and conscripts could have been pushed into building works in Egypt.

The Book of Exodus opens with the Israelites in Egyptian captivity; led by Moses, they escape. The role of Moses is complex. He is a fugitive, a receiver of revelation, a tough politician, a successful leader of his people who liberated them sometime towards the end of the thirteenth century.

The group of escapees had a religious experience on Mount Sinai and a solemn covenant was ratified between God and his people, Exod 19. The rest of the Book of Exodus, Leviticus, Numbers, Deuteronomy unfolds the laws of the Covenant in the context of the journey to the Promised Land. The Pentateuch ends with the death of Moses on the eve of the people's entry into their possession.

The group eventually arrives in Palestine. It establishes relationships with others of a similar background. In the end, each other's experience and history becomes a shared heritage. An early statement of Hebrew belief opens with the words, 'A wandering Aramaean was my father', Deut 26:5. The style of life built into this statement of belief left its mark on the Israelite frame of mind and suggests the origins of the Israelite system of belief.

They were a travelling people. Ancient biblical tradition makes a clear distinction between the Israelite patriarchs and the indigenous population of Canaan. It points to a migration from the Northeast as the reason for their presence in the Canaanite area.

In terms of critical historiography efforts to reconstruct the origins of the Israelites are largely guesswork.[1] Some of the ancestors may have settled the land through the Bronze Age making the seasonal migration to graze the flocks. Others may have been part of the Semitic population that inhabited the land as far as the records go back. Some may be the disaffected Hapiru known from the Amarna letters. These were dispatches sent to the Egyptian government in the first half of the fourteenth century BCE. Some may have been escaped slaves from Egypt or Philistinian migrants. However, a nomadic group arriving in the land imprinted their distinctive ethos on the population.

This migration has been linked with movements of the Amorite peoples in the Middle Bronze Age. These people brought a new vision of God, society and the role of men and women. The central ingredient in the religion of the Amorites was the relationship between a covenanting tribal deity and his people. He led his people as they wandered from place to place in search of pasture or trade. God's life, then, finds its expression in the experiences of his people rather than the seasons, the rainfall, the corporate institutions of settled life.

Likewise, it was the tribe rather than the city that gave a meaningful context for living. A striking example of this can be found in the prominence of genealogy. The genealogies have their own special role in Genesis and generally establish a continuity. They are found elsewhere in the OT and in the Gospels. A genealogy has its base in the life of nomadic tribes.[2] The basic form of social life among nomads is the tribe or family. Accordingly, the genealogy establishes relationships, roots and family networks and so it is the statement of belonging. Family history becomes less important when a tribe becomes sedentary. Identity is now found in authority, forms of authority, the foundation of states, civic and religious institutions, places.

When the biblical traditions were collected and codified, the nomadic past was a distant memory. Even still, however, history rather than place defined the identity of the people. This became all the more important when exile and emigration re-entered their experience.

Indeed, the cosmos itself finds meaning in history. This mindset is clearly evident in the creation accounts of Genesis 1-3. The creation of the cosmos leads to the existence of the first man and woman as the climax of the process. Creation is the human environment and exists for human wellbeing. In itself it is not threatening; it is good. The stars do not determine existence. They light the world and mark the seasons. Human beings are not absorbed into the cycle of nature, finding meaning therein. They are the stewards of God. The divine creative activities are described in terms of emerging clarity, substance and division. Chaos gives way to light; solid land appears through the turbulent treacherous waters; sentient beings are divided into species. The process of clarification continues when Adam names them. They become significant as integrated into his life. Humanity brings meaning to the universe rather than receives its meaning from it. So a tiny people confront the age-old worldview of the surrounding peoples with quite a new understanding.

The sense of journey through time and place finds its fullest expression in the Exodus experience. It was the Exodus journey that shaped the vision of Judaism for all time. Far more happened than a mere deliverance from bondage. The liberated people entered into a pilgrimage that would lead them across not only physical barriers but also countless frontiers of mind as they struggled to live a hope filled life in many and varied circumstances. The Covenant that lies at the heart of the Exodus experience was their inspiration. Through it God makes permanent the relationship implied in the single event of the Exodus. God delivered this people: but now he binds himself to be always their deliverer. God showed his love and mercy then; now he binds himself to be always loving and merciful. At the same time their behaviour is subjected to definite standards. All future Israelites will enjoy the same activity of God.

The Deuteronomic History

History writing is a process of selection and interpretation. The process depends on one's starting point and what one feels is important. Carr writes, 'The facts are really not all like fish on the fishmonger's slab. They are like fish swimming about in a vast and sometimes inaccessible ocean; and what the historian catches will depend, partly on chance, but mainly on what part of the ocean he chooses to fish in and what tackle he chooses to use – these two factors being, of course, determined by the kind of fish he wants to catch. By and large, the historian will get the kind of facts he wants'.[3] In a manuscript written in 1936 Collingwood says, 'St. Augustine looked at Roman history from the point of view of an early Christian; Tillemont, from that of a seventeenth-century Frenchman; Gibbon, from that of an eighteenth-century Englishman; Mommsen, from that of a nineteenth-century German. There is no point in asking which was the right point of view. Each was the only one possible for the man who adopted it'.[4] This process is seen at work in the Deuteronomic history.

In 1943, a scholar called Martin Noth advanced the theory that a number of Old Testament books were originally one. These would be Deuteronomy, Joshua, Judges, 1 & 2 Samuel, 1 & 2 Kings. There is a continuity of theme and style in these writings. The author gathered already existing traditions and skilfully constructed his own framework and bridging material. He used much older material to convey a particular understanding of Israel's history. The Book of Deuteronomy that began the work supplied the theological vision that animated the rest of it and shaped the presentation of material. The original author believed that Deuteronomical theology was the key to understanding the history of the period covered. According to Noth, the work was put together during the exile in Babylon because it finishes with the release of King Jehoiachin from prison in Babylon in 561 BCE. The work was composed to help the exiles understand how they ended up in exile. Their plight was the result of their ancestors' unfaithfulness to the Covenant as set out in the laws of the Book of Deuteronomy.

Noth's theory has been refined and elaborated in various ways. It has been seen that not just one editor but a series of them have worked on the tradition over a period of time. However, they were guided by the same basic insight and the theory still holds.

Deuteronomy, therefore, was a theological preface and the interpreting principle with which to view all subsequent history. The literary form of the book is in terms of Moses' last farewell address to his people. The people had now reached the end of their long period of wanderings. They stood poised at the frontiers of Palestine ready to invade it. Yet Moses who led them for so long is not to see the completion and goal of his work.

Deuteronomy attempts to answer fundamental questions. Why should God choose one people? What sort of response is expected? It teaches the doctrine that keeping God's laws should be the expression of an inner attitude of love, loyalty and a warm desire to obey.

In Deuteronomy, the divine action that instituted the covenant is described for the first time as an act of election. 'For you are a people holy to the Lord your God, and the Lord has chosen you to be a people for his own possession, out of all the peoples that are on the face of the earth', Deut 14:2. This election resulted in the gift of the land, Deut 9:4-5 and the gift of the law, Deut 4:40; 5:33; 6:2, 18, 24; 11:9; 12:28; 13:17, 18. The laws were designed to increase the health and prosperity of the people. As seen here, the law is in no sense a burden; it is an expression of grace. The fundamental law is clear. 'You shall love the Lord your God with all your heart, and with all your soul, and with all your might', Deut 6:5. Because of this, there is determination that the law must be taught to children and never forgotten, Deut 6:5-9. Loyalty to God brings emphasis on purity of religion and unity of worship. There is to be one sanctuary and that is to be in Jerusalem, Deut 12:5-14. The options are clear. 'See I have set before you this day life and good, death and evil', Deut 30:15. If they follow the law they will prosper; if they do not they will perish, Deut 30:16-18.

The subsequent historical books are organised around this guiding vision. Gerhard von Rad writes, 'The most varied traditions, the belief in election (of a chosen people), the tradition of the patriarchs, the traditions of Moses and the revelation of God on Mount Sinai, and many other things have been fused in Deuteronomy into a unit of such encyclopaedic scope and of such a rigid theological uniformity as was never again possible for the faith of Israel. One does justice to the significance of this theological accomplishment only if one understands that there had never been such a compilation of the traditions of all Israel at all before Deuteronomy. Formerly the individual Israelite lived in obligation to one of the holy places and to the regulations and traditions practised there. Deuteronomy, however, is in earnest with its belief in the indivisible Yahweh (6:4), who can be worshipped in only one sacred place by one Israel. Deuteronomy injected this understanding into a period in which everything, the political as well as the religious existence of Israel, was in complete dissolution'.[5]

The first of the historical books, Joshua, describes the conquest and occupation of the land. The success of the people is seen as a blessing from God. Joshua 1 and 22-24 make this point very clearly.

From the twelfth to the eleventh centuries, the land was populated by three main groups: the Hebrew tribes, the Canaanites and the Philistines. The tribes were more a cultural than a political unity that was occasionally threatened by the Canaanites, the Philistines and raiders coming in from the desert in the East. In times of crisis, a charismatic leader would appear who would unite at least some of the tribes against the enemy. Such leaders were called judges and well-known figures would be Deborah, Gideon and Samson.

The book of Judges covers this period. Samuel is the last of the judges. He features in the first book of Samuel, which describes the resistance to the Philistines and the eventual decision made around 1020 BCE. to choose Saul as the first king. The pattern of infidelity, punishment, repentance and peace is the organising framework of the history.

The second book of Samuel begins around the year 1000 b.c.; Saul is dead and David becomes king. The expansion of his empire is described, as well as David's triumphs and failings and the court intrigues in Jerusalem. The time of David was seen by the editors as a time of fidelity and blessing. David was succeeded by Solomon, who ruled over Israel from 962–922 BCE. The first twelve chapters of 1 Kings describe his building programmes, foreign alliances and the wealth of his kingdom.

1 Kings 12-22 and 2 Kings cover a period of over three hundred years and it is a story of increasingly rapid decline. The decline is punctuated by brief periods of partial recovery and reform but ends in total annihilation with the revival of the Eastern imperial nations of Assyria and Babylon. This was also a time of significant economic change in which the patterns of Israel's communal life were further affected by social imbalance and alien religious influences.

Solomon died in 930 BCE. Within days the structure erected by David fell apart, to be replaced by two rival states of second-rate importance. They existed side by side; sometimes in friendly alliance, sometimes at war. They were the northern and southern kingdoms. The northern kingdom took the name of Israel. The remnant in the south that remained loyal to the Davidic dynasty became known as Judah.

Judah was smaller, poorer: therefore there was less social tension. The population was homogeneous, being largely Jewish. It was geographically isolated and therefore could escape the attentions of armies looking for prey. Finally, it had political stability; it kept up the dynastic succession within the house of David. Israel was larger, wealthier and therefore prone to social division and the unwelcome attentions of foreigners. There was a large Canaanite population and this gave rise to religious problems. It was geographically more exposed to outside influences. In Israel, new dynasties were often formed with the family members of the previous dynasty wiped out by the newcomer.

The Northern Kingdom survived until 721 when it was finally destroyed by the Assyrian armies from the East.

Judah fell to Babylonian invasion in 587 BCE. Jerusalem was plundered and largely destroyed with the deportation of many of the leading citizens.

Some decades later, the exiles gathered together their historical traditions to form the final version of the Deuteronomic history providing an explanation of all that had happened. Their judgement on the history of the peoples from the death of Solomon onwards is generally negative. The northern kings are all condemned; only two of the southern kings are approved, Hezekiah, 2 Kings 18:3-7 and Josiah, 2 Kings 22:2. The disasters that had befallen the people can be understood. They were the appropriate punishment for the peoples' failings. However, a reading of Deuteronomy still contains the seeds of hope. God's fidelity and forgiveness is constant, Deut 1-3. They will seek him again and they will find him, Deut 4: 29-31, 30:1-10.

The Chronicler's History

In October 539 BCE the Persian leader Cyrus took over Babylon without a fight. He now had brought the whole of the Babylonian Empire under his control. In pursuit of a policy of allowing subject peoples to enjoy cultural autonomy within the framework of the Empire, the Jews were allowed to return home in 538 BCE.

Dedicated adventurous spirits went back while others financed the venture from exile, Ezra 1:2-4; 6:3-8. Building the new community was slow and difficult. Seventy years after the first return, Jerusalem was still thinly populated and remained largely in ruins. The newcomers faced years of hardship, privation and insecurity. Intermarriage with pagans meant that the lines separating Jew and Gentile began to blur and there was a real danger that much of what was authentically Jewish would be lost.

In the second half of the fifth century, a gentile called Ezra arrived. He was charged by the Persian king with the task of regularising Jewish religious practice. Sometime later Nehemiah came to rebuild the walls of Jerusalem.

The books of Chronicles, Ezra and Nehemiah share a common purpose. They intend to give theological backbone to the problems of living as a small subject nation, without freedom or king, in a vast multi-cultural and multi-racial empire. This theology develops in the context of a representation of their history from Adam to the coming of Nehemiah. According to Boadt, 'It was the beginning of a profound change that gradually shaped Israel into what can be recognised as the beginnings of modern Judaism. The Books of Chronicles stress the role of the cult, prayer, worship and ritual purity as a way of life. Ezra the scribe began a shift toward separateness. Holy things are reserved to the priests and levites, marriage with Gentiles is forbidden, and loyalty to the Torah in its written form of the Pentateuch becomes mandatory. Nehemiah reinforces this sense of exclusive status by completing the walls of Jerusalem and forcing people to live within the city and treat it as the centre of the Jewish hopes.'[6]

The Chronicle tradition sees the establishment of the Temple cult as essential to survival. With that in view it rewrote the life of David giving him a great zeal for worship, composing many psalms and establishing guilds of priests and levites, with their own roles, to serve in the Jerusalem temple. Ezra broke up all marriages to pagans, Ezra 10:3, and reaffirmed the laws about sacrifice, ritual purity, and worship, Neh 8-9. Nehemiah built the walls of Jerusalem making the city a safe and secure location for the temple, Neh 2:17.

History and the Covenant
The history that unfolds in the Bible is very unfamiliar. The text itself can seem archaic, strange and primitive needing all the tools of historical research, linguistics, archaeology, and literary criticism to tease it out fully. However, the study of the Bible is not an attempt to recover a museum piece. Encased in this ancient material is the raw passion of real faith engaged with the ever-living God. It describes a gracious God establishing a community with his people and their efforts to live and believe faithfully in many times and places. As long as men and women walk this earth, the Biblical scenario is of eternal relevance because everyone's experience is captured, explored, addressed and questioned there.

This relationship is summed up in the word 'covenant'. Israel came from a milieu in which the gods were the object of mistrust and uncertainty. A covenant showed them exactly where they stood with this God. It reassured them that at least under certain specified circumstances they could have confidence. The ethos of the creation accounts is clearly the by-product of this. Love and trust are characteristic of the covenanting God to those who are faithful to his ways. Psalm 25:10, 'All the paths of the Lord are kindness and constancy towards those who keep his covenant and his decrees'; Jn 1:14. There is no basic kinship between God and this community; the covenant was inaugurated out of the compassion of God for an enslaved people. Its continuance depends on the consistency of character of this God who had chosen them: there is constant reference to the *hesed*, steadfast love, and faithfulness of God. See especially Ex 34:6f., 'The Lord, the Lord a merciful and gracious God, slow to anger and rich in kindness and fidelity, continuing his kindness for a thousand generations, and forgiving wickedness and crime and sin'. The various laws and regulations associated with the divine appearances in the exodus tradition are attempts to spell out for Israel the implications of this covenant relationship. Eichrodt sums up the significance of the Covenant, 'First a clear divine will becomes discernible, which can be depended upon and to which appeal can be made. The covenant knows not only of a demand, but also of a promise: 'You shall be my people and I will be your God'. In this way it provides life with a goal and history with a meaning. Because of this the fear that constantly haunts the pagan world, the fear of arbitrariness and caprice in the Godhead, is excluded. With this God, men know exactly where they stand; an atmosphere of trust and security is created, in which they find both the strength for a willing surrender to the will of God and joyful courage to grapple with the problems of life'.[7]

This is a good statement of the reality of covenant life. Its basis is a supremely free act of divine love. God chose them not because they had anything special to offer, not because of their importance in the international scene, but out of his love. 'For you are a people consecrated to God your Lord. It is you that Yahweh our God has chosen to be his very own people out of all the peoples on the earth. If Yahweh set his heart on you and chose you, it was not because you outnumbered other peoples: you were the least of all peoples. It was for love of you and to keep the oath he swore to your fathers that Yahweh brought you out with his mighty hand and redeemed you from the house of slavery, from the power of Pharaoh king of Egypt', Deut 7:6-8. As a result they become the very special possession of God. In response they vow to serve him.

The Covenant, which is the fundamental instrument and expression of God's dealings with his own, was made with a wayfaring people; they were in exodus. On the way, they met God. The way itself, ever changing, but never without direction, was the context in which Yahweh revealed his purposes. As the pilgrimage of Sinai became the pilgrimage of history, the people sought to grasp the divine will by drawing together the past, the present and the future. They were confident in doing this because their religious experience taught them that the changing world was a place of grace, freedom and rationality. There is no trace of remorseless fate or pure chance in their perception of reality. The stability of their faith rested on established patterns of justice and mercy rather than structures or dogma. This sense of purposeful movement will find expression in apocalypse and eschatology, the teaching of Jesus and the Christian vision of a church in pilgrimage to the future.

2.2   THE GOSPELS

Gospel and community

In the year 112 CE, Pliny the Younger was the Emperor's representative on a special commission in the province of

Bithynia and Pontus. This province lay along the southern coast of the Black Sea. While there, an extensive correspondence was carried on between himself and the Emperor. In one such letter to Trajan we get some idea of the strength of Christianity in that area: '... a great many individuals of every age and class, both men and women ... It is not only the towns, but villages and rural districts too which are infected through contact with this wretched cult ... temples almost entirely deserted for a long time; the sacred rites ... allowed to lapse ... flesh of sacrificial victims ... scarcely anyone could be found to buy it'.[8] Here is evidence of the astonishing growth and strength of the Christian faith in a relatively short period of time. A sense of its wildfire expansion is conveyed in the following text, 'In those first days there was no doubting the effect Jesus had. Twenty years after the crucifixion of Jesus his story was already being told in the great cities of the eastern Mediterranean. It spread like a forest fire and people everywhere were caught up in it. They formed groups, and became a kind of Jesus movement. They met together regularly, and claimed that they were commemorating his death. It might seem strange that anyone could keep going back to something as grisly as a death by crucifixion. Yet that is what these people did as they met together, drawn from all walks of life, educated and uneducated alike. They said that the crucified Jew in distant Palestine had totally transformed and renewed their lives.'[9]

The Christian mission was not directed to any one sector of society. Early Christianity was very mixed in its social composition. This follows on from the methods of Jesus, himself. 'One of the remarkable characteristics of Jesus' ministry is his ability to move in and out of various status groups: peasants, townspeople, tax collectors and prostitutes, ... Pharisees and well-to-do urbanites'.[10]

A number of changes took place in the Christian fellowship in the generation after the death and resurrection of Christ. It changed from being a Jewish movement to a Gentile one; and

Gentiles were allowed into the Church without first becoming Jews. The difficulties and tensions generated by this development are well illustrated in the Acts of the Apostles and the Epistles of St Paul. The second obvious change was when it moved from a rural to an urban environment. 'The dominant imagery of the Gospels is rural, and the occupations of the Twelve tend to be those of the countryside .... The rural imagery of the Gospels is replaced in Acts by scenes set in urban synagogues and city streets, harbour waterfronts and government courtrooms and jails'.[11]

Apostles, disciples of Jesus, charismatic travelling preachers and traders and workers moving from city to city on their business, carried out the missionary task in the post-Paschal period. Paul is described as making his first contacts in the synagogue, Acts 17:1-2. According to himself, however, his first interest were the Gentiles, Rom 1:5; 11:13-14; 15:16; Gal 1:16; 2:2,7-9. We read of Paul 'having daily discussions in the lecture room of Tyrannus', Acts 19.9. In Rome he evangelised from his own 'rented lodgings', Acts 28:23,30. He spoke publicly at Athens, Acts 17:17-34. 'For the most part, however, converts first heard the message on the more intimate scale of personal contact, through friends and acquaintances who then took them to one of the group's weekly meetings'.[12] The usual Christian group was small, being limited by the size of the house in which it met. They gathered on a regular basis on Sundays, Acts 20:7; 1 Cor 16:2. The Eucharist was a customary feature of these meetings, Acts 2:42; 1 Cor 10:14-22; 11:17-34. The owner of the house functioned as host or patron, Acts 18:7-8; Rom 16:23; 1 Cor 1:16; Col 15. The fact that they lived in a vast cosmopolitan empire emphasised the universalism of their mission and frequent visits and written communications bound the various cells together. Hospitality in receiving Christians from other churches was accordingly emphasised, Rom 12:13; Heb 12-13.

The early Christians called themselves 'brothers' and 'sisters'. The Pauline letters give a sense of unity of these groups. 'The letters ... reveal that those groups enjoyed an unusual degree of intimacy, high levels of interaction among members, and a very strong sense of internal cohesion and of distinction both from outsiders and from "the world"'.[13] In this context, division between Christians was all the more scandalous, 1 Cor.1:10-16. A characteristic and conspicuous feature of these communities was their concern for those who were in need. This features strongly in the teaching of Jesus, Mt 19:16; 25:31-46. There are frequent references to the same theme in other New Testament writings, Acts 6:1; 9:36. Rom 12:13; Heb 13:1-3; Jas 2:14-16; 1 Jn 3:17.

The Gospel as oral form

When Jesus was teaching, he used the same method as every gifted teacher of his time. His listeners had no paper; they had to carry his message in their heads. So he would talk and at the end of a period of talking, tell a story or craft a saying which they would memorise. That was the origin of the stories like the parables and the sayings of Jesus in the Gospels.

The sayings, stories, miracle accounts were used again and again in the day-to-day life of the Christian community. From repetition there emerged a stereotyped way of presenting various scenes from his life and a standardised collection of sayings. This material was communicated and organised for practical use. As a result, the time sequence and locale of the teaching and events were generally lost. As needed, the individual preacher quarried a saying or an event from the Community's rich tradition. In the process, the fact that this saying was pronounced before or after that event was largely forgotten. So we can understand the rather curious appearance of the material, a series of loosely connected paragraphs lacking any real chronological sequence.

The science of *Form Criticism* examines the history of this material in the pre-literary stage, that is, the circumstances in which the individual units were used, their 'setting in life'.

Some sayings and stories were used for teaching about prayer; others about relationships and so on. Form criticism also classifies the units into various literary forms or types: miracle stories, sayings, parables; finally, it studies the evolution of the material at this period of oral transmission. Did it change much?

Historical narrative or testimony of faith?

The next question is: what sort of a 'genre' is a Gospel? Is it biography or theological treatise? This antithesis has dogged Gospel studies for most of the twentieth century.

In the old days, it was a simple fact and perfectly evident that the Gospels were biography. The Gospels were lives of Christ. In 1924, Hilarin Felder could tot up the evidence: apostolic authority, eyewitness evidence, interest in giving the facts, accurate; and conclude, 'the Gospels are ... in their full extent and in the strictest sense of the word, historical authorities and scientific evidence'.[14]

The death knell for this approach was already sounded in 1906. For a century or more scholars had attempted to recast the Gospel material in a form acceptable to the modern reader. This involved a process of historical research, manipulation of sources, creativity and selection. The progress of the movement – book by book, and author by author – was charted by Albert Schweitzer in his The Quest of the Historical Jesus, English edition (London: Adam & Charles Black, 1910). His conclusions were devastating. The Jesus that emerged from this process had little or no basis in history at all; he was a modernisation; a product of nineteenth-century version of the ideal human person and good behaviour.

In 1926, the German scholar Rudolf Bultmann wrote, 'I do indeed think that we can now know almost nothing concerning the life and personality of Jesus, since the early Christian sources show no interest in either, are moreover fragmentary and often legendary; and other sources about Jesus do not exist'.[15] Bultmann's starting point was a distinction he made between the Christ of faith and the Jesus of history. The centre of faith was the Risen Christ, alive, here and now, the Christ of faith. He contended that the early Church had little or no interest in the facts of the life of the historical Jesus. The sayings, stories and narratives of the Gospels reflect the interests of the early Church and are set and formed in the context of preaching, prayer, catechetics and apologetics. They reflect these interests and are not an account of an actual life.

The original question was – are the Gospels biography or theological treatise? They are a bit of both. There is no doubt that the Gospel authors sought to present a real man and they were interested in the historical Jesus. This is clear from Lk 1:1ff; 1 Jn 1:1ff. It would be very strange indeed if human curiosity alone did not seek out information about his life. It has been argued that the first believers rather quickly lost whatever interest they had in an earthly Jesus. This would demand an extraordinary about-face to explain the origins of the Gospels. Could they believe in a shapeless Lord without an effort to give a profile, a substance to his presence, which would come from knowing his earthly teachings and activities? Over and above this, the life of Jesus was itself the content of the preaching. Jesus was not just remembered as a teacher of timeless truths, but his person was as central as what he did. As they saw it, theological insight was shaped by events and words that actually happened and were said. We see that concern in the experience of Paul himself. In Gal 1:18 we read that Paul went to Jerusalem to visit Peter. As St Jerome wrote, he did not go to Jerusalem 'to look at Peter's eyes, cheeks and face, to see if he were fat or thin, whether his nose was hooked or straight, whether he had a fringe of hair across his brow or was bald'.[16] The Greek verb 'historesai' 'can mean 'to visit, to get to know, to inquire about, to gather information (from someone)'. There are reasons for thinking that the last meaning is appropriate in Gal 1:18, namely, that it was on this occasion that

Paul gained some of his detailed knowledge about Jesus'.[17] This interest in the facts of things is seen in the role given to teachers and the prominence of tradition. In the beginnings of the church in Antioch, the two most important ministries were prophets and teacher, Acts 13:1. In the list of 1 Cor 12:28, teachers come next after apostles and prophets in order of rank. The financial support of teachers is noted in Gal 6:6. A central task of these teachers must have been the preservation and instruction of the Christian tradition. That is what teachers do. They preserve accurately to instruct faithfully. The importance of accurate transmission is seen in the emphasis given to tradition in the New Testament. Paul writes on the traditions he passed on to his Churches, 1 Cor 11:2; 15:3; Col 2:6; 1 Thess 4:1; 2 Thess 2:15; 3:6. The Jesus tradition and respect for it is evidenced by texts such as those found in 1 Cor 7:10, 12, 25 where a clear distinction is made between Paul's own teachings and the teachings received from the Lord. The way in which this tradition first began is clear enough. In a less literary culture the use of memory to preserve the records of the past can be highly developed. In the case of Jesus, as with many of the rabbis of his time, the punch lines of his talks were crafted as such and memorised. The parables of Jesus, and his sayings and miracles were part of the preaching kit of the twelve and the seventy-two long before the death of Jesus. These formed the Gospel tradition. James Dunn writes, 'In short, the idea that the first Christians were not interested in the pre-Easter Jesus is little short of ludicrous. On the contrary, they would certainly have been concerned that the memories of 'all that Jesus said and did' should be passed on to new converts and retold in new churches'.[18]

Yet this brings us to the second point: the history goes hand and hand with theology. The Gospels were written to help us encounter the saving, mastering Christ-Redeemer. Relevance as well as history determined the shape of the Gospels. This literature is not the detached, clinical or regretful account of a life nobly lived and now done. Christ was not a figure of the past, but an exalted Lord whose presence surrounded the evangelists' contemporaries on all sides. Historical witness was the window into a man who was intensely involved in their own lives. As the early Christians saw it, the saying 'your sins are forgiven' was not part of the records of yesteryear, but a contemporary event to all who called on Christ in faith. This will have its effect. The Risen Lord had totally changed the lives of the preachers, teachers and believers and so they relate the Gospel material to their matured experience of Christ and his Church. They nuance this, colour that, expound a doctrine in greater detail. We must remember that the Gospel authors are not reporting what Jesus said and that alone. They are transmitting what Jesus once said and is now saying to a believer whose life was radically changed by the Lord. In bridging the gap between *once said* and *now saying* they will tend to take the words and events of Jesus' life and relate them to their own situation.

The implications of this for Gospel composition are clear-cut. The Gospels are lives of Jesus. They are lives, however, which preserve the significant material at the expense of details that have no real relevance. If the Gospel narratives seem austere they are so because those vivid details that normally lighten the written page are absent. What remains is a text that can speak to the lives of all people, irrespective of time and place.

It would be difficult to explain the existence of the Church in the last third of the first century apart from the explanation that they give themselves. The Gospel portrait of the life and activities of Jesus seems the best available. Could the Church exist without a man such as Jesus, without a career more or less as we find it in the Gospels, without a teaching as presented by the evangelists, and finally, without a resurrection experience which transformed a shattered community into a group of vibrant hope? While it is evident that the Gospel authors have put the stamp of their individual personality on their materials, yet one clearly discernible individual, Jesus, escapes all their organising and control, to shine brightly through. The same personality is found in all four. His sayings have an unmistakable stamp of sharpness and originality. His stories are vignettes of astonishingly evocative power. His activities are unexpected and unconventional. There is a swift and direct mind whose processes transcend all those around. There is a personality that burned itself on the memory of those in contact with it.

The Gospel as literary form

For some twenty-five to thirty years the Gospel material existed in an oral communication. It was preached and taught to the faithful. No need was seen to write it down. As the English scholar Vincent Taylor puts it in a striking phrase, 'The time is one in which precious fragments are treasured for their immediate interest and value; Christian hands are full of jewels, but there is no desire to weave a crown'.[19]

The units existed in the faith and life of the community: proclamation, catechesis, liturgy, controversy, and prayer. The centre of this tradition was a Living Lord; when they recounted snippets of his teaching or events from his life they were not trying to recapture a lost Camelot or hearken back to some golden age, but trying to listen to and understand that Jesus whose knock on the doors of their life they experienced every day. With that in mind a nineteenth-century scholar chiselled out the epigram, 'No apostle, no New Testament writer, ever *remembered* Christ', J. Denny (1895).

As the first century went on, many communities were founded in city after city. In the life and diversity of these communities, the value of an authoritative written text was quickly evident. This is all the more so when we consider the nature of Christianity itself. The first preachers did not present themselves as great thinkers or philosophers expounding timeless doctrines or ideologies. Rather, they spoke of events and happenings in their own lifetime, and therefore, their message was a news, a good news, 1 Jn 1:1. This basic conviction was the stimulus for Gospel composition. As the first century drew to a close and the first generation of preachers began to die off, it became vitally important to preserve their testimony, Jn 21:24.

The more widespread Christianity became, the greater the need for a document. In the homelands of the faith a living tradition and recollection reached back into the life of Christ. This was not so abroad! A document was a basic instrument for unity of belief and communion. 'A growing church, for example, would need to cover, with its authoritative materials about Jesus, a wider geographical range than the custodians of such memories, the apostles and their immediate followers, could responsibly cover. Again, as new converts began to proclaim their faith, some check would be needed on the accuracy with which they presented the material about Jesus of Nazareth. The disappearance through death of those who had known Jesus, and who served as the wellspring and check on the traditions about him, may have also served to add impetus to the desire to have some organised presentation of the traditions about him. The Pauline letters, and the earlier traditional materials they contain (for example, Phil 2:6-11, a pre-Pauline hymn or confession of faith) emphasise Jesus as pre-existent, and as risen and regnant, with almost no reference to the deeds and words of Jesus' earthly career. A desire awakened by hearing Jesus thus proclaimed, to know more about him during his period as man in Palestine may also have contributed to the final creation of the literary form which we know as "gospel"'.[20]

The formation of the four Gospels
The Gospels were written in the same spirit as the transmission of the tradition, 'from faith to faith', to convert others, to

introduce them into the world of life, meaning and fulfilment that the authors themselves experienced.

One Gospel author gives some information on the procedure leading to the composition of a Gospel and his aim, Luke 1:1-4. He notes three levels of transmission:

- At the base is the historical reminiscence of those who were eyewitnesses and ministers of the word. The link between 'eyewitnesses' and 'ministers of the word' is significant. They witness to what they have seen and heard. It is a seeing and hearing that through faith penetrates to the deeper dimensions of the historic events. It is only by a combination of faith and physical experience that they can become ministers of the word.
- The second level is the task of those 'many' who recorded 'just as ... delivered'. One of the many would, of course, be Mark.
- Finally, there is his own contribution.

His method, 'having investigated from the source all things accurately' (the Greek verb for 'investigated' is *parakoloutheo*.), means that his care and thoroughness is obvious; his intention at least was to go about things in an orderly way; his text has a shape to it. The verb *parakoloutheo* can also mean to observe, to be in close touch with, to participate in events, or 'having being familiar with' – a variation noted in the Arndt and Gingrich Greek lexicon.[21] If this is an introductory unit to Luke-Acts as a combination, both meanings can be retained. 'In regard to the gospel material Luke has 'investigated;' matters in detail. He has done the same thing for Acts, but with the advantage that he has more immediate knowledge of more recent events, and has actually participated in some of them himself'.[22]

The point of it all is the 'truth concerning the things of which you have been informed'. The knowledge is already his. It is a question of conveying, 'in a *permanent* and *assured* form what he has previously learned in a less systematic manner.[23]

It is difficult to underestimate the genius of the creators of the Gospel narrative. They gathered and organised the material and in the process invented a new type of literature. After a long analysis of possible literary parallels to Mark, the first evangelist, Howard Kee concludes, 'Accordingly, we must agree with the judgement of Amos Wilder: "(The Gospel) is the only wholly new genre created by the Church and the author of Mark receives the credit for it".'[24]

Redaction Criticism

In the high noon of form criticism, the role of the actual authors of the Gospels was diminished and they became the flat, anonymous collectors of traditions with their importance and influence effectively nil. Typical expression of this way of thought is found in the following observation penned in 1919, 'The literary understanding of the synoptics begins with the recognition that they are collections of material. The composers are only to the smallest extent authors. They were principally collectors, vehicles of tradition editors. Before all else their labour consists in handing down, grouping, and working over the material which has come to them'.[25]

The beginnings of a leak in this attitude are already dribbling back in 1901. That year saw the publication of W. Wrede's *The Messianic Secret in the Gospels*. He tracked down a hitherto unsuspected influence exerted by Mark on his traditional raw material. A theme of misunderstanding runs through Mark – the disciples display a relentless obtuseness in their dealings with the Lord. Allied to this is the doctrine of the messianic secret: whenever the disciples approached a true understanding of Christ, he enjoined silence. According to Wrede all this flows from the mind of Mark and represents the evangelist's attempt to explain the failure of so many to grasp and commit themselves to Jesus. In the relatively recent past, this insight has been taken up in a branch of studies called **Redaction Criticism** or editorial criticism. A ground-breaking

essay was that of G. Bornkamm. 'The Synoptic writers show –
all three and each in his own special way – by their editing and
construction, by their selection, inclusion and omission, and
not least by what at first sight appears an insignificant, but on
closer examination is seen to be a characteristic treatment of
the traditional material, that they are by no means mere
collectors and handers-on of the tradition, but are also
interpreters of it'.[26]

This puts an emphasis on the theological role of the
evangelists; they are not just purveyors of traditions; they are
not just historians; they put their own stamp on their materials.
Evidence for this is found in how they used traditions; the
patterns and sequence of the units; the seams or link passages
that they composed; the alterations and emphases which they
put into the units they wrote down.

Form criticism spoke of the life setting of the units of
tradition. With redaction criticism we must pursue the life
situation of the Gospels as completed whole in the
communities for which they were written. What was going on
in these communities? What was the evangelist getting at? Why
did he couch the material with this particular slant? Pioneer
work has been done in this area by Marxsen on Mark;
Conzelmann on Luke and Bornkamm on Matthew.

The Evangelists and their Communities

Mark

The Gospels were written in response to the needs of various
Christian communities. The value of the texts in presenting
systematic and permanent information on the life and teachings
of Jesus is obvious. However, the issues that engaged these early
churches can differ. This is clear from the slant and presentation
of the individual Gospels as the evangelist selects from the
tradition of stories, sayings and events from the life of Jesus what
was relevant to their own situation. The science of redaction

criticism helps us understand the interests and approach of the individual evangelist and through that the needs and questions of the audience that will hear and read his text.

The issue of suffering was of major interest for the community which first received the Gospel of Mark. The evangelist tailored his presentation accordingly. The disciples were silenced when they approached a deeper insight into the meaning of Christ, Mk 8:30. They were not allowed full expression of their faith until they had seen the crucifixion. Their difficulty in coping with this idea is presented with dramatic flair, Mk 8:33; 9:32; 10:32. Faith in the mystery of the Lord had to be combined with the acceptance of his death. This death is seen as the supreme revelation of his meaning and was first grasped by the pagan Roman centurion. 'Truly his man was the Son of God', Mk 16:39.

To be a disciple of Christ is to share in his sufferings, Mk 8:34; it is to give oneself as Jesus did; to be greatest is to be first in service, Mk 9:35. This leads to an unfettered, free and open life, Mk 8:35.

Matthew

There is an important body of Jewish converts in the community of Matthew's Gospel. This explains the emphasis on the fulfilment of Jewish expectations in Christ. There are also Gentile converts, and Christ commissions his disciples to preach to all nations. The references to harassment and persecution reveal the stresses that the community was subjected to. Believers were insulted and libelled, 5:11. They are being persecuted hated, 13:21; 10:22. Christians are arraigned before the Gentile courts for their beliefs, 10:18. They are even being put to death, 24:9. The Jews had a hand in their persecution. They are flogged in the synagogues, 10:17; 23:34. They are in danger of death, 10:28.

The community has an internal organisation, 16:18 and has the means to make binding decisions on its members, 18:15-20.

Under the pressures of persecution, some have fallen away, 13:21. They have even betrayed one another, 24:10. False prophets are leading some astray and love is growing cold, 24:12.

Confronting this situation, the evangelist presents Christ as the presence of God among us, 1:23; this presence will be with his community until the end of time, 28:20. Discipleship will lead the believer into many a storm, but Christ is with his community, 8:23-27.

Luke

He inserts the mission of Jesus firmly into human life and history. The birth of John the Baptist took place during the days of Herod, king of Judea, Lk 1:5. The birth of Jesus is connected with a decree of a Roman emperor, Lk 2:1-2. The ministry of John the Baptist begins in the fifteenth year of the reign of the emperor Tiberius (28–29 CE), and during the prefecture of Pontius Pilate (26–36 CE), Lk 3:1. He notes that at the time another Herod was Tetrarch of Galilee and Philip was Tetrarch of Ituraea and Trachonitis and Lysanias tetrarch of Abilene. The high priests were Annas and Caiphas, Lk.3:1-2. Events touching the early Christian community are associated with the famine during the reign of Claudius, Acts 11:18; the expulsion of the Jews from Rome (49 CE), Acts 18:2; and the Proconsulship of Gallio in Achaia, (52 CE), Acts 18:12.

In the Acts of the Apostles the ministry of Jesus is continued in the Christian community. The foundation members had to have a full experience of the historical ministry of Jesus, Acts 1:15-26. On the three occasions when the conversion of Paul is described, the Church is described in terms of Jesus living in the world, Acts 9:4; 22:7; 26:14.

The community that received this Gospel were converts from paganism to the Christian faith. This is indicated by the lack of interest in Jewish issues. While using Mark as a source, he omits the controversy about what is clean or unclean, Mk 7:1-23. He replaces the Jewish title 'rabbi' with 'lord' or 'master'

– compare Mk 9:5 and 10:5 with Lk 9:33 and 18:41. In the genealogy placed at the beginning of the Gospel the descent of Jesus is traced from Adam, Lk 3:38 rather than Abraham as in Matthew's Gospel, Mt 1:1. Luke places the Lord in the context of universal humanity. It seems clear that he was writing for a largely Gentile community.

Nevertheless, he is clear on the Israelite roots of the Christian mission. The birth of Christ and his mission are firmly placed in the Biblical world of promise / expectation / fulfilment. He will be the expected Davidic king, Lk 1:32-33; Simeon sees him as a long awaited Messiah, Lk 2:26-32. The theme of fulfilment is clear in Jesus' first synagogue teaching: 'Today, this scripture has been fulfilled in your hearing', Lk 4:21. After the resurrection, on the road to Emmaus the meaning of Jesus is teased out in the light of biblical teachings, 'everything written about me in the law of Moses and the prophets and the psalms must be fulfilled', Lk 24:44.

The fulfilment, however, takes an unexpected direction. There are clear social concerns. Christ in Luke's Gospel is the friend of the oppressed, the poor, women, gentiles, whoever is looked down upon, downgraded or oppressed. The beatitudes in Luke are addressed directly to the deprived: 'Blessed are you who hunger now', Lk 6:20-21. Only in Luke does the Baptist instruct the tax collectors and soldiers on just practice, Lk 3:12-14. It is the hated and foreign Samaritan who gathers the injured Jew in his arms, Lk 10:30-37. Women play a prominent role in his Gospel. Among them are Mary, Elizabeth, the sisters at Bethany, Lk 10:38-42. The Christian fellowship involves a sharing of resources, Acts 2:44-45; 4:32-37.

The community is continually energised by the power of the Holy Spirit. The first words of Jesus in the Gospel are, 'The Spirit of the Lord is upon me, because he has appointed me to preach the good news to the poor', Lk 4:18. The Holy Spirit comes upon Mary, Lk 1:35 and the disciples at the first Pentecost are possessed by the Spirit, Acts 2:4.

John

The Fourth Gospel was written towards the end of the first century. A long tradition associates it with a Christian community that lived in the port city of Ephesus, which is on the west coast of the country we now call Turkey.

In their prayer and reflection, the believers there had a sustained focus on the divine mystery of Christ. This, however, gave rise to an alarming trend. The humanity of Jesus was in danger of being swallowed up by his divinity and the fact of the incarnation was seen as of no account. One of the purposes of the Gospel was to counter this tendency. 'The Word became flesh and lived among us', Jn 1:11.

The wonder of Christ is precisely the fact that the divine mystery is present and manifest in the life, words and actions of a fully human person. That is why Jesus is called Word in the Fourth Gospel. He is the living revelation of God and what is revealed is love, Jn 3:16. Christians are to reflect that love in their own communities, Jn 17:11,21.

The way in which God touches human life and fulfils its needs is deftly conveyed in the seven 'I am' statements 'I am the bread of life' Jn 6:35, cf. Jn 8:12; Jn 10:4; Jn 10:9; Jn 10:11; Jn 11:25; Jn 14:6; Jn 15:1.

The evangelist notes the role of the Holy Spirit in the reflective activity of the community with particular care. According to Jn 14:16 the Holy Spirit is involved in the remembering of Christ's words and actions as they are pondered again with new levels of insight, Jn 12:16. Through the Spirit Christ talks to the believers as through the ages they attempt to grasp the mystery in different situations, Jn 16:13-14. A link between the Spirit and worship is made in Jn 4:43, 'and those who worship him must worship in Spirit and in truth', a living prayer, prompted by the Holy Spirit and directed by true teaching.

An Introduction to the Synoptic Problem

The first three Gospels, Matthew, Mark and Luke are very much alike, so much so they can be arranged in parallel columns and be compared with one another. At a glance, the reader can then see their similarities and differences. This process of looking at them together has given them the name Synoptic from the Greek word *'synopsis'* that means *seeing together.*

There was a large body of tradition relating to Jesus in circulation by word of mouth. All this could be drawn up by the Gospel authors and, according to one, not a fraction of the material was actually written down, Jn 21:25. With such rich resources, the Gospels have the potential to be very different from one another. This is not so. Centuries of comparing the first three Gospels have revealed a measure of agreement between them that can only be explained on the basis of literary interdependence. The words used, the sequence of units are too close to allow any other conclusion. The similarities are clear. However, the problem is complicated by the fact that they differ from one another as well. The challenge of explaining all this is called the synoptic problem. The examination of the synoptic problem attempts to construct a hypothesis that will explain the similarities and the divergence. The agreements are evident. Whereas the Fourth Gospel has a three-year public ministry, the whole thing takes place over a period of twelve months according to the synoptics and the order of events is much the same. The ministry of Jesus begins with a short period by the River Jordan and the wilderness where he is baptised and tempted. This is followed by the ministry of preaching and healing around the Sea of Galilee with Capernaum as its base. This is followed by the journey to Jerusalem, the Last Supper, Trial and Crucifixion. The similarities would be clear in the parallel texts, Mt 9:1-17; Mk 2:1-22 and Lk 5:17-39, which describe in the same order unrelated events, using much the same words – the healing of the paralytic at Capernaum, the call of Levi and the question of fasting. The same can be seen in the calming of the storm, the Gerasene demoniac and the cure of the daughter of Jairus, Mt 8:18-9:34; Mk 4:35-5:43; Lk 8:22-56. Another example would be the sequence made up of the confession of Peter, the first prediction of the passion, the Transfiguration, the cure of the epileptic, the second prediction of the passion, Mt 16:13-17:23; Mk 8:27-9:32; Lk 9:18-45.

The differences are also evident. There is material that is only found in Matthew. An example of this would be the account of the birth of Jesus, Mt 1-2. A number of parables are also unique to Matthew. These would be the parables of the weeds, Mt 13:24-43; the hidden treasure and the pearl, Mt 13:44-46; the dragnet, Mt 13:47-52; the unjust steward, Mt 18:21-35; the labourers in the vineyard, Mt 20:1-6; the two sons, Mt 21:28; the guest without a garment, Mt 22:11-14; the ten virgins, Mt 25:1-13; the talents, Mt 25:14-30; the sheep and the goats, Mt 25:31-46.

Material found only in Luke would be for example the infancy narratives in Lk 1-2 and some very well known parables – the parables of the prodigal son, Lk 15:11-30, good samaritan, Lk 10:29-37, pharisee and publican, Lk 18:9-14, rich man and Lazarus, Lk 16:19-31.

Again, Matthew and Luke share material that is not found in Mark, about 250 verses. An example would be the Sermon on the Mount. This is found in Mt 5-7 and distributed throughout Luke chapters 6, 11,13,14,16. Several passages are almost identical, for example: Lk 6:41-2 and Mt 7:3-5; Lk 3:7-9 and Mt 3:7-10. The Lord's Prayer is found only in Mt 6:9-13 and Lk 11:2-4. However, its format is very different in these two sources.

Where did they get this extra material? We can rule out the possibility of one drawing on the other directly for the following reasons:

- Why did they omit material that is proper to one or the other if one was the source of the other?

- Even the material that they have in common can differ significantly in sequence and in content.

This source that Matthew and Luke have in common is normally called 'Q' (from the first letter, it seems, of the German word *'Quelle'* meaning 'source' or 'spring'). It is often described as the Q-document. The contents are usually estimated at about 220-235 verses or parts of them. This document would be the source drawn on for much of the moral teachings of Jesus as found in Matthew and Luke. A good example of this is the memorable Sermon on the Mount that is found substantially in Matthew and Luke. Yet it is difficult to call it a single document because fairly substantial differences can show up as it is used by Matthew or Luke. Perhaps, it might be more accurate to call it the Q-tradition. This would be made up largely of the sayings and teachings of Jesus.

There is no solution to the synoptic problem that can accommodate all the difficulties. However, the following solution solves most of them. Mark was written first and Matthew and Luke had the following sources.

1. The Gospel of Mark.
2. Another source which in some way or another they have in common.
3. Sources that are individual to Matthew and Luke.

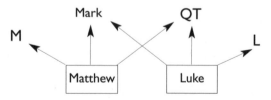

In this diagram, Mark and the Q-tradition are seen as the sources for Matthew and Luke. M and L represent sources that were available to Matthew and Luke individually.

3

The Literature of the Bible

There can be many types of literature. The word often used is 'genre' – history, biography, poetry, tragedy, comedy, romance, essay, and letter, for example. When reading a piece of literature it is important to be clear about the genre because that will determine the way the text is understood. A novel cannot be read as history, poetry cannot be read as prose and so on.

We have already touched on the variety of genres that are found in the Bible. The Bible is a book of books (as described in p. 3 and the comment on literary criticism in pp. 9-10). A number of genres are found in the Bible: myth, story, novel, letters, apocalypse, poetry, wisdom, and prophecy, each of them with the characteristics of its type.

In this section we will look at three ways in which the Bible communicates its message: by story, reflection, and symbol.
Story can take several forms. The narration of a people's past is the story of its history. Novel, novella and parable are fictitious story with a clear message coming through the presentation.

The language of **reflection** is the process whereby a people attempts to crystallise its feelings, understanding, hopes and dreams through the medium of poetry.

Religious language presents a particular challenge. It attempts to capture realities that are beyond immediate human perception. In many ways, the truth escapes the ways in which we try to picture it in words. In this context, the use of very precise language is dangerous. It can convey a clarity that is misleading. The looser, more evocative language of **symbol**, myth and epic is more appropriate. These are media of communication that attempt to say something real and at the same time convey the conviction that the realities dealt with transcend the means of human communication.

The most profound religious thinkers have a deep sense of the limitations of their knowledge and an openness to the insights of other faith traditions. Conversely, a superficial clarity distorts religious truth and can lead to fanaticism and intolerance.

3.1   THE LANGUAGE OF STORY

The importance of narrative in the life of a community

'Once upon a time' are perhaps the most comforting of all words with their memories of snuggling down, floating away into the world of imagination, dreams and sleep. Good stories speak to our minds unfolding deep insight; they also speaks to our feelings, imagination, experience. Generations of young people were nurtured by the collections of stories from Hans Anderson, the Brothers Grimm, *Tales from the Arabian Nights*. For many of us, fundamental insights into life were communicated to us by these milestones in our learning process; just as for generations children's sense of wonder and communion with nature has been developed by Jemina Puddleduck, Peter Rabbit and Mrs Tiggy-Winkle, and modern children lose themselves in the world of Harry Potter!

As we grew more mature some of the great classical novels developed our sensibilities. Such is the power of their story that they open our minds to whole new ways of feeling for life, the individual, society and one another. In a similar way, family bonding is strengthened when we tell the account of our individual lives and family lineage. In the formation of national self-consciousness, a most potent force is the narrative of one's country's history with all its struggles, stories, epics and mythologies. In relatively modern times, and only in some cultures, abstract language has been used to channel insight, philosophy and understanding. For the greater period of human history, such information was transmitted by myth, story, and epic.

What is the strength of the Bible? The language of the Bible is concrete rather than abstract. Its potent impact lies in the fact that the narrative of people vis-à-vis events is a far more gripping force in the lives and imaginations of a community than the statement of abstract principle, no matter how profound it might be. Principle and syllogism might convince us of a truth; story excites us with a truth, compels and grips our attention. In the transmission of the faith it is necessary to draw out the meaning of the stories and narratives of our faith. We organise this into creeds and doctrines but, in the process, much is lost. The sorting is done according to the modes of thought of a particular time. In moving to doctrinal proposition much of the echoing, inviting depth of the story/narrative is lost. John Shea writes, 'They are stories meant to disclose aspects of our relationship to God and through that relationship our commitments to each other. The stories of scripture were remembered and today remain memorable because they are similar enough to our own lives for us to see ourselves, yet different enough from our lives for us to see new possibilities. They tell us what we want to know and more. They come close to home and yet are an invitation to a journey ... The traditional stories, both historical and fictional, reflect concerns and conflicts present in our lives and suggest ways of dealing with them'.[1]

At the centre of our faith is the story of a people. It covers over a thousand years. In their coming together in the land, they became a model for the lived experience of many peoples down through the ages escaping from harsh, repressive regimes. They discovered the guiding hand of God in the evolution of their history, moments of triumph, reversals, war, peace and exile. The demands of social living, justice, mercy and faithfulness became the arena of encounter with divine mystery. The God-directed heart might wish to divert itself into the comfortable rhythm of ritual, but was forced to involve itself in history because that is where God is taking into himself the pain and oppression of every son and daughter of the nation.

The story of Jesus is placed in the context of all the previous stories. They give him a background, while he in turn reconfigures all the stories that went before him. The story of his life contains many of the stories that he told himself. 'In all this Jesus spoke to the crowds in parables', so writes St Matthew, 13.34. He goes even further with the observation, 'indeed, he would never speak to them except in parables'. Jesus was an extraordinarily effective storyteller knowing that in the long run the human mind absorbs more from narrative than proposition. At the heart of Christian prayer and worship is the endlessly retold story of Jesus, who unmasks the mystery in ordinary human life, Jesus 'who hugs kids, cries over a friend's death, and tells homely stories from everyday Palestinian life – and all the while unveiling the effable mystery and love that permeate them all'. [2]

The story of Job

The Book of Job is constructed as a dialogue between Job and three of his friends. It is about the problem of evil, human behaviour and the justice of God. It is a dramatic account of the limitations of all human thought when trying to grasp the reality of God and the mystery of life. It is cast in the form of a story-dialogue with a remarkable interplay of feelings and emotions.

The book seems to have two sources. There is a traditional tale of a just man who was tried and vindicated by God, chapters 1-2 and 42:7-17. Into this an author has placed his own composition, 3-42:6.

The structure of the book is very clear. It opens with the story of Job's life and how God tested him, 1-2. There follows a conversation between Job and three friends, Eliphaz, Bildad and Zophar. They discuss divine justice, and the suffering of Job. This ends with Job demanding that God should defend his justice, 3:31. A fifth character called Elihu appears and insists that Job and his friends should just accept the divine control of the situation without question, 32-37. God appears and proclaims his mystery beyond human understanding, which shows up the pride and arrogance of Job. Job submits, 38-41. The book ends with Job restored to his former greatness and his friends are condemned for accusing him, 42:7-17.

This central section from chapter 3 to 42:6 is a profound, painfully challenging exploration of human innocence, suffering, divine justice and power. Any glib answers are challenged.

In the beginning Job patiently accepts his adversity: 'God gave, God has taken back. Blessed be the name of God', 1:21.

From chapter three on, the atmosphere changes. Job begins to rebel and question. People believed that God was just; he was good and all-powerful. In this scenario the good will prosper and the evil be punished. Eliphaz expounds on that position, 'Think now, who that was innocent ever perished? Or where were the upright cut off?', 4:7. His friend, instead of supporting Job, is saying that he has himself to blame for his predicament.

Job is not having any of this. It does not measure up to the facts. He knows that he has lived a good life. He vigorously rejects the opinion that his sufferings are the result of his sins. He knows that he is innocent. His knowledge is not a theory.

He knows the truth about himself. He invites Eliphaz to stop thinking in the abstract and really look at Job himself, 'But now be pleased to look at me; for I will not lie to your face', 6:28.

He becomes upset, full of anger towards God and bitterness about his situation. 'Therefore I will not restrain my mouth; I will speak in the anguish of my spirit; I will complain in the bitterness of my soul', 7:11.

The other friend, Bildad, has no time for Job's complaints. 'How long will you say these things, and the words of your mouth be a great wind?', 8:2.

Job responds and has a moment of great bitterness. 'It is all one; therefore I say, he destroys both the blameless and the wicked', 9:22.

God forcefully challenges Job with all his foolish questions: 'Brace yourself like a man; I will question you and you shall declare to me. "Where were you when I laid the foundation of the earth?"', 38:3. In the description of the wonders of creation that God planned and knows, the limitations of human knowledge become clear.

Face to face with God, Job admits the inadequacy of his insight. 'Behold I am of small account; what shall I answer thee?', 40:4.

However, prayer does bring one into a personal relationship with God. In the process Job grasps his own littleness and the limitations of human understanding. 'I had heard of thee by the hearing of the ear, but now my eye sees thee; therefore I despise myself, and repent in dust and ashes', 42:5. Face to face with God in personal relationship, the sufferings do not seem to be of any great account anymore.

Even though the questions are not answered, there is a happy ending of sorts in which Job comes through his doubts and learns to trust in God. The author leaves us with his acceptance of a divine plan which is simply too vast for him to understand.

Some of the questions that Job raises will find a solution as revelation develops. In all, the book is a trenchant attack on superficiality. There is no depth to those who fail to see the complexity of human situations and the mystery of God.

Parable as genre

In the New Testament, the term parable can have several meanings. In Lk 4:23, a proverb is called a parable. 'Doubtless you will quote to me this parable, 'Physician, heal yourself'.' In Mk 7:15 a saying of Jesus is described as a parable. However, as we use the term 'parable' here, it refers to the stories of Jesus.

In general these stories fall into three types. The first would describe an event from real life (like finding a lost coin, Lk 15:8-10 or the seed growing to a full harvest) and draw a message from it. Another would tell a vivid fictitious story. Examples of this would be the persistent widow and the unjust judge, Lk 18:1-8; the sower, Mk 4:3; the debtors, Lk 7:41. In these two types a parallel was drawn between two different things, in one case a widow demanding justice from the judge and the individual in persistent prayer; in the other seeking the lost coin and seeking the kingdom. The final category would include stories that are examples of the general principle, rather than parallels. The good Samaritan, Lk 10:29-37, for instance, is an example of what it means to be a neighbour.

A parable is a short story with a main point. The details are more or less realistic trimmings of no great significance except as a build up to the story. In general, a parable is distinguished from an allegory where all the details have meaning. However, some parables have allegorical elements.

There are universal characteristics in story telling that are present in the parables. 'The rule of contrasts', virtue and vice, riches and poverty, good and bad, wisdom and folly are sharply contrasted. Another is the 'Rule of three' and, so, the three travellers in the good Samaritan story, the three excuse makers in the great supper, and the three servants in the Talents.

Some parables of Jesus

These stories are the product of a master storyteller whose language reveals an ability to look keenly and appreciatively at the world around him, 'consider the lilies of the field'. Indeed, if we gathered together all his images, we would have a reasonably detailed description of daily life in ancient Galilee. Climatic events feature, the weather and the changing seasons, the breeze that stirs the reeds, the sky rose-red at sunset or at dawn, the lightning flashing from end to end of the heaven, the wadis in spate under the lashing rain, and the crops withering under the burning sun. Sometimes the image is chosen from growing things, the lilies of the field, the darnel weeds in the patch of wheat, the mustard seed expanding into a shrub, the tiny flowering herbs of mint and cumin; other times he draws from the world of animals, domestic and wild: sheep, goats, pigs and dogs, oxen, asses and camels, wolves, foxes, snakes and scorpions; and from the birds, the hen with her brood of chickens, ravens, doves and sparrows, vultures wheeling in the sky. Human occupations are called upon endlessly: the steward working over his accounts, children playing in the market-place, the ploughman, the gardener and the builder all busy at their work; then there are the burglar, the robber and the embezzler, people busy threading needles, patching cloths, sifting wheat, filling wine-skins, grinding meal, making bread, catching fish and mending nets. Even in the Gospel of St John we have the wind whispering over the land, the fields white for the harvest, the grain of wheat dying, the vine and its branches, sheep stealers, the shepherd grazing and folding his flock, tending his sheep and lambs. He made the whole world a sacrament of his teaching.

It is important to situate the parables in their wider context, the coming of the Kingdom of God and its beginning in Jesus' own ministry. This Kingdom of God is neither the Church nor heaven. It is God active within life. The emphasis is on the power of God here and now breaking into peoples' experience and calling them to decision for or against the divine challenge.

In various passages Jesus alludes to people's difficulty in understanding the parables, Mk 4:11-12. For them the story would be easy to follow; what eludes them is the point of the story. This meaning escapes those who are unwilling rather than unable to grasp it. When Jesus questions his disciples about the parable of the Sower, he says, 'Do you not understand this parable? How then will you understand all the parables?', Mk 4:13. These words imply that they should be able to understand. A parable does not state its point with absolute clarity; it needs the engagement and effort of the hearer and that engagement comes from good will.

The Parable of the Sower, Mt 13:1-9.
It is a story of growth. The general context of this parable is the coming of the kingdom of God, the difficulties it encounters and its ultimate triumph. The story was first crafted during Jesus' preaching in Galilee. He was not achieving much success. The parable explains his confidence in spite of adversity and encourages his disciples as they in turn encounter indifference, persecution, and lack of commitment in their efforts to share the Good News.

At that time, the seed was sown before the ground was ploughed. It was not just carelessness that led the sower to scatter the seed on the path, the rocks and the briers. He had intended to plough the path. Prior to the ploughing, the rocky patches and the brier roots would have remained unnoticed. The rocks would be covered by a thin crust of earth and after the heat of the summer the briers would have withered back to their roots.

The message is that in spite of many setbacks, the power of God, the coming of his kingdom, will produce a full and final success. This success will be immeasurably greater than anything expected.

Such a story is addressed to those whose faith and hope are under pressure. The farmer is undaunted by failure; he is not defeated and in the end he has a bumper crop. The parable of the Sower is designed to lift the spirits of Christians in difficult times in the twenty-first as in the first centuries.

The Gospels append an explanation of the parable, which gives a different emphasis, Mt 13:18-23; Mk 4:14-20; Lk 8:11-15. This time the stress is not on the power of the Kingdom reaching certain success. It is on the dispositions of those who listen to the Word of God. Some are inattentive and careless. Others take it seriously. Many scholars would contend that this second interpretation arose in the early years of the Christian Community.

The Parable of the Labourers in the Vineyard, Mt 20:1-16
Jesus spoke about the coming of the Kingdom of God. It touched everyone's life, the great and the little, the good and the bad, Jews and Gentiles. Nobody was excluded from God's all-inclusive love. Jesus not only spoke about this issue; he embodied that coming in his actions. He associated with people from all walks of life and was bitterly criticised for it. We read that he shared food with the despised, and the shunned tax-collectors and sinners. He received them and ate with them. This drew down the ire of the religious elite, the Scribes and the Pharisees, Lk 15:2.

The parable is divided into two parts. In the first part, Mt 20:1-8, the labourers are hired. Five groups of them are taken on at different times of the day. With the first, the householder agrees on a wage, one denarius, which was a normal day's wage at the time. He promises to pay the others 'whatever is right'. In the end, he pays them all one denarius. The second part, Mt 20:11-16, records the grousing of those first hired and the response of the householder.

In the story, it is the time of the grape harvest. Autumn is at hand; the rainy season is near; speed is of the essence and so the vineyard owner goes out on several occasions to the hiring place in a constant search for workers.

Nobody was treated unjustly. A wage had been agreed with the first wave of workers. What was striking was the exceptional generosity of the employer.

The whole story is a protest against the unjustified, loveless and unmerciful attitude of the Scribes and Pharisees. By contrast, this story of exceptional care shows what Jesus is about and that is what God is about. God has equal care for the littlest and most needy.

Jesus is reviled, on a regular basis, because he is a companion of the despised and outcast. He replies by saying this is what God is like, full of compassion. The central words in the story of the vineyard owner are Mt 20:16, 'Why be envious because I am generous'. He pays those who have worked a long day; this is just. In the sheer generosity of a compassionate and sympathetic man, he pities those who come last and have nothing to take home with him. This is an attitude that has nothing to do with economics, but is based on the understanding of a Loving God!

The Ten Wedding Attendants, Mt 25:1-13

The context of this story is the coming of Christ and the need to be ready for him. The previous chapter, Mt 24, contains one of the Gospel apocalyptic texts on the coming of Christ and the close of the age, Mt 24:3. The early Christian believers believed that this coming would take place in their own lifetime. The time to get ready was very short. This belief gave rise to some unexpected practices. St Paul had to reprove some people for their idleness. They saw no point in work if Christ was going to reveal himself in the immediate future, 2 Thess 2:2; 3:11-12. The years rolled by and there was no sign of Christ manifesting himself. With the lapse of time, the urgency to prepare for him also diminished.

The image of a wedding feast is used elsewhere in the Gospel to convey the sense of celebration and joy that the fullness of the kingdom of God will bring, Mt 22:1-14. The point of this parable is to generate or regenerate an attitude of alertness. Jesus is urging his disciples to ready for the appearance of God in their lives whenever it may take place. The plaintive cry of the maidens 'Lord, lord, open to us', Mt 25:11, is a reminder of those in Mt 7:21 who were also refused admission to the kingdom of God because they were not doers of the word.

There is little information available on Jewish wedding celebrations in the first century. Descriptions are available of Arab weddings at the turn of the last century. Early twentieth century Palestinian customs cannot be used to reconstruct what happened most of two thousand years before. At the same time they are interesting and might indicate traditions that emerge in the parable. The bridegroom came to the bride's house close on midnight. Lit by candlelight the pair and their friends went off to the bridegroom's father's house where the marriage ceremonies and further entertainment took place. Both the reception of the bridegroom with lights and the hour-long waiting for the bridegroom's arrival, are frequently mentioned in modern reports of Arab weddings in Palestine. Even today the usual reason for delay is that agreement cannot be reached about the presents due to the relatives of the bride. To neglect this often lively bargaining might be taken to imply an insufficient regard for the relatives of the bride; on the other hand, it must be interpreted as a compliment to the bridegroom if his future relations show in this way that they give away the bride only with the greatest reluctance'.[3]

Which or whether, the emphasis is on preparedness, the closing of the door and the refusal of admission to the five who were not sufficiently ready.

The museums have thousands of examples of the kind of lamps used. These were small earthenware vessels. They had a spout through which the wick was drawn. Extra oil was carried in jugs. The girls are not condemned for falling asleep. Neither are the five blamed for not sharing the oil, better five with lighting lamps than none at all. Behind this last detail might be an allegorical element. Wise use of time and personal commitment are all-important. Christians cannot rely on others for fulfilment.

In the story there is no mention of the bride and the ten virgins evidently stand for the Christian community. Five were wise and five were foolish. This is in line with Matthew's understanding of the Church: the people with whom Christ is present are not a select, elitist group. He recounts Jesus' stories of the cockle, Mt 13:24-30; and the fishing net Mt 13:47-50 and the mixture that attended the wedding feast, Mt 22:1-10. The community is a mixture of good and bad that Christ will sort out in the end.

The Unjust Steward, Lk 16:1-13

Face to face with the coming of the Kingdom and God's judgement, believers are challenged to make wise and prudent decisions. This is what this parable is all about.

In the story, the steward was accused of wasting his employer's resources. He has betrayed his trust and faces dismissal. His only option was to ingratiate himself with the debtors with a view to receiving future favours from them.

He acted decisively, and changed the accounts, and the master approved of his foresight and commended him for his sensible actions.

One of the first questions is who is the master in question? It would seem unlikely to be the employer. How could he possibly praise the steward for embezzling his own property? The master in question could be Jesus commenting on the story and recommending his disciples to be as wise in unworldly issues. It may seem strange that Jesus commended fraudulent conduct, but the fact that the steward was dishonest was irrelevant to the story. Jesus was only interested in praising his resourcefulness. In this case the parable would have ended in verse 7. From 8 on are a series of sayings of Jesus commenting on it and related issues.

There is another way of interpreting the story. Demanding a cash interest on money lent was against Jewish law at the time. A common way of getting around this prohibition was to seek interest in kind and not in coin. The interest could be paid in oil, corn or other goods. Although against the spirit of the law, the custom just about scraped past the letter of the law. This is what the steward was up to. He lent his master's goods, but charged and pocketed an interest that had to be paid in goods, not money. In changing the promissory notes, the master still got his capital back, but the steward forfeited his profit. The steward therefore undid what was really illegal, remained in the good graces of the debtors and did his master no harm either. Indeed, the cancellation of the interest would probably improve the master's good name and make him look generous.

This puts another slant on the story. Undo what is illegal and against God's law; amend evil ways and remain in God's good graces.

In the period of the oral tradition, to assist the memory, sayings of Jesus were grouped according to theme. The story of the unjust steward is about worldly possessions and linked to it are further sayings on the same theme.

There is a clear note of sarcasm in the recommendation that worldly friends can provide an eternal hospitality, verse 9.

There are two sayings on dishonesty, verses 10 and 11.

Luke has a clear doctrine that possessions are for communal use. They belong to others. If one is not faithful to that ideal, the personal higher gifts, which are true riches, will not be received either, verse 12.

The unit concludes with two statements on divided loyalties, verse 13.

3.2   THE LANGUAGE OF REFLECTION

The purpose and language of poetry

How does the craft of poetry work? It is a process whereby a felt insight is captured in a way that can be transmitted to others and other generations. By means of metaphor, tone, sounds and rhythm, poetry holds the atmosphere of mood, feeling, and experience. It is a linguistic union of ideas and their expression that is controlled by the poet. Seamus Heaney writes, 'The poem was written simply to allay an excitement and to name an experience, and at the same time to give the excitement and the experience a small perpetuum mobile in language itself.'[4]

Poems can touch on the whole range of human experience. It can be social issues. In the tightly structured meter of *The Rape of the Lock*, Pope conveys the topsy turvy disarray of values in his society when husbands and Lap-dogs are made equal. The fair Belinda is distressed when the Baron cuts off her lock of hair:

> Not louder Shrieks to pitying Heav'n are cast,
> When Husbands or when Lap-dogs breathe their last,
> (111:157-158).

In 'Dover Beach', Matthew Arnold grippingly conveys a world that is chaotic and meaningless and bereft of hope:

> And we are here as on a darkling plain
> Swept with confused alarms of struggle and flight,
> Where ignorant armies clash by night.

When asked is it impossible for a poet to move out of his political context, the Ulster poet John Montague replied, 'It would be dishonest if he did – not only to his own past but to his family's past as well. What's in his blood must speak through him. He must bear witness, as Ritsos and Amichai and Neruda have done. But in a context of understanding, compassion, diagnosis, hope'.[5] His anger at the loss of Gaelic civilisation is clearly expressed in his poem, 'The Rough Field'.

> I assert
> a civilisation died here;
> it trembles
> underfoot where I walk these
> small, sad hills:
> it rears in my blood stream
> when I hear
> a bleat of Saxon condescension.

Human love is memorably celebrated in Shakespeare's sonnet:

> Shall I compare the to a summer's day?
> Thou art more lovely and more temperate.

From the most ancient times men and women have attempted to immortalise their insights and feelings in poetry. Since we are what we know, our horizons are widened when we know great poems. There is much poetic material in the Biblical tradition, but it is in the book of Psalms that faith receives its fullest expression in that medium.

The poetry of the Psalms
It is estimated that about one-third of the Hebrew Bible is poetry. The poems are found in the wisdom books of Job and Ecclesiastes; they are part of the prophetic books and Proverbs and Lamentations. The Book of Psalms would be the major poetic collection. Since they are poems, the psalms must be read as such. Poems have their own logic and language with emotional connections, hyperbole, use of rhythm and mannered development.

The Psalms were written by many different poets. They were composed over a period of time. One hundred and fifty of them are gathered in one book of the Bible called the Psalter.

What sort of poetry are they? It is difficult to establish the kind of metrical structures that might exist in the Hebrew psalms. The original stress patterns are lost in translation. However, the rhythm of the Hebrew text is largely carried by parallelism that is preserved in translation. Parallelism is a favoured technique where a line is paired with another and there is a balance of sentences. Sometimes both are saying much the same thing in different words. A good example of this would be, 'He who sits in the heavens laughs;/ The Lord has them in derision', Ps 2:4. 'O come let us sing to the Lord/ let us make a joyful noise to the rock of our salvation', Ps 95:1. Other times, it repeats the theme through its opposite, Ps 35:1. Many variations are possible, but the parallelism highlights a theme; gives it greater impact; introduces a reflective pause in the development of an idea and completes the rhythm of the unit. It is a literary technique that features often in the sayings of Jesus giving them a balance 'for with the judgement you pronounce you will be judged, and the measure you give will be the measure you get', Mt 7:2. What we have in these cases is rhythm of sentences rather than a metre. A metre gives a rhythm of words and syllables. In the case of parallelism, the meaning of the sentences rather than the sound gives the swing. Two types of parallelism are mentioned: synonymous and antithetical. Synonymous parallelism says the same thing twice using different words. An example of synonymous parallelism would be found in the first verse of Ps 2.

Why do the nations conspire
and the peoples plot in vain?, Ps 2:1.

The antithetical form of parallelism is found in Ps 1:6. In this case the second line contrasts the first.

> for the Lord knows the way of the righteous,
> but the way of the wicked will perish, Ps 1:6.

As well as the parallelism, an economy of words, terseness of expression would be characteristic of this poetry. Metaphor is also used:

> I am like a desert-owl in the wilderness,
> an owl that lives among ruins.
> Thin and meagre, I wail in solitude,
> like a bird that flutters on the roof-top, Ps 102:6f.

A number of the psalms have an acrostic pattern. These are Pss 9-10, 25,34,37, 111,112,145. In this case, it means that each line of the psalm begins with the next letter in the Hebrew alphabet. The Ronald Knox translation of the psalms is one of the few that attempts to reproduce this in English.

> At all times I will bless the Lord; his praise shall be on my lips continually.
> Be all my boasting in the Lord; listen to me, humble souls and rejoice.
> Come, sing the Lord's praise with me, let us extol his name together.
> Did I not look to the Lord, and find a hearing; did he not deliver me from all my troubles?
> Etc. Ps 34:1-5.

The idea behind this method is to help memorisation and give a sense of completeness, the A to Z of the issue has been covered.

The psalms grew out of the day-to-day experience of the people and cover a wide range of themes and experiences.

There is praise of God. There is thanksgiving for deliverance from danger, false friends, and sickness. Other psalms are prayers for the wellbeing of the community and its leadership. As poetry, the psalms have a universality of appeal that makes them relevant to any age and any people. 'If the Old Testament psalms have not merely survived but remained alive and in use for thousands of years, the reason is that in them there has been preserved a way of calling on God which is spontaneous and direct and by means of which man can speak to God as he really thinks and feels'.[6]

Herman Gunkel (1862–1932) pioneered the modern literary analysis of the Psalter. He classified the psalms according to various themes. Some psalms escape classification; modifications of his system have been proposed. However, Gunkel's grouping of the psalms gives some idea of their content and so his classification can be helpful. He divided them along the following lines.

Hymns or songs of praise

It is instinctive in the human person to praise what we value, and invite others to join in that praise. 'Wasn't it a wonderful performance!'; 'Isn't she marvellous!'. When the psalmist invites us to praise God, he is working from a profound conviction that God's loving will underpins all creation and the fortunes of his people and individuals.

These psalms tend to begin with an invitation to praise God. The call is directed to oneself, Ps 103-4, or the community, Ps 117.

The motive for praise is then given. 'The Lord is merciful and gracious', Ps 103:8. The reason could be the wonder of creation. 'Yonder is the sea, great and wide, which teems with things innumerable, living things both small and great', Ps 104:25. The cause of praise could be the fidelity and justice of God, 'who executes justice for the oppressed; who gives food to the hungry', Ps 146:6-7.

These psalms often end with a repeated call to praise. 'Bless the Lord, O my soul! Praise the Lord', Ps 104:35.

Thanksgiving Psalms

The general movement of thanksgiving psalms is quite like that of the songs of praise, except in this case the psalmist calls for thanksgiving and then outlines what he is thankful about.

In Ps 118 he begins with the words, 'O give thanks to the Lord, for he is good; his steadfast love endures forever!'

He then describes his own personal experience of God's care. 'Out of my distress I called on the Lord; the Lord answered me and set me free'.

Psalms 18, 105, 107 are on a similar theme.

Lamenting Psalms

These psalms can express an individual lament or a communal one. Most of these psalms, however, are an expression of personal loss and tragedy. They begin with a cry to God for help. 'How long, O Lord? Wilt thou forget me forever? How long wilt thou hide thy face from me? How long must I bear pain in my soul, and have sorrow in my heart all the day?' Ps 13:1-2.

This is followed by a description of the psalmist's distress. This can take many forms: it might be sickness and death, Pss 6:5. Persecution is the problem in Pss 38:12-20; 41:5-11. He asks for forgiveness from sin, Ps 51. In most cases, as in Ps 13:3-4, the language used is so generic that the psalmist's problems are not too clear. This is to the advantage of those using them as they express the distress of the human heart in many different situations.

Apart from Ps 88, these psalms end in a note of confidence. 'I will sing to the Lord because he has dealt bountifully with me, ' Ps 13:6.

Royal Psalms

These could have been occasioned by a royal wedding, Ps 45, a royal coronation or anniversary, Pss 2, 72; they could be prayers before, Ps 20, or after military operations, Ps 21, or even a royal thanksgiving, Ps 18. These were preserved even when the monarchy had ceased after the fall of Jerusalem 587 BCE. They survived because they were interpreted in Messianic terms, remembering the promise of 2 Sam 7: 13, which is specifically alluded to in Pss 89:4 and 132:11. In this new context, the king and the Davidic dynasty became symbols that God would send a Saviour who will lift his people up.

Royal Psalms which celebrate God as King

Another group celebrates God's rule over his people. Some scholars would believe that there was an annual celebration of God's rule over the people and the world. Psalms that celebrate the kingship of God and his rule over the waters of the sea and the storm would fit this context, Ps 47; 93; 95-99.

Because of King David's musical accomplishments, 1 Sam 16:25, he is associated with many of the psalms. However, there is no convincing evidence that he composed any of them. It seems clear enough that the psalms were originally used in Temple and public worship. The musical notations indicate that they were sung. 'To the choirmaster' is a comment that begins many psalms, for example Ps 13. The accompanying instruments are specified, flutes, Ps 5; stringed instruments, Pss 4, 54,55,61,76. The tune of a song called 'The Lilies' is to be used for Ps 80.

3.3   THE LANGUAGE OF SYMBOL

Much of religious language is symbolic. It has to be, because it deals with the human person in relationship to what is not immediately perceived by our senses in ordinary experience.

Theological language is analogical. It points to realities a fragment of whose truth is caught in our day-to-day language. The words we use suggest rather than define the content of its statements. We describe God as light, shepherd, or father (which he *is*, but not in the ways in which we commonly experience these realities). As a result, religious language is acutely conscious of its limitations and the fact that it is open-ended, with one symbol suggesting another and none capturing the whole truth.

Religious language is the language of experience and participation. It is not a product of detached, scientific observation. Because we have actually experienced God as shepherd, when casting around for a word to describe this our mind seizes the term shepherd. In turn, the language of religion is designed to establish moods, feelings, and persuasive motivations leading to action. Rather than detachment it leads to commitment; more than analysis, it generates encounter.

Examples from literature of the use of symbolic language
Symbolic language is a type of pictorial expression. It is designed to engage feelings and the imagination as well as the mind. The strength of symbol or metaphor is vividly experienced in poetry. In 'Dover Beach', the Victorian poet, Matthew Arnold, airs his views on human misery in the symbol of a seascape. The 'grating-roar' of the pebbles rising and falling with the waves 'bring/The eternal note of sadness in'. Another nautical metaphor is used by Tennyson in 'Crossing the Bar'. The 'bar' is the sandbar at the mouth of the harbour. Crossing the bar is a symbol of death. 'I hope to see my Pilot face to face/When I have crossed the bar'. For Shelley, the soaring, singing skylark becomes a symbol of poetic inspiration at its best. 'Teach me half the gladness/That thy brain must know,/Such harmonious madness/From my lips would flow/The word should listen then – as I am listening now'. Keats' dream of unfettered poetic inspiration finds symbolic expression in a bird as well, this time

the nightingale. 'Thou wast not born for death, immortal Bird!/
No hungry generations trod thee down'. The 'living stream' is
the symbol of life in Yeats' poem, 'Easter 1916', while timeless
beauty is symbolised by Byzantium in *Sailing to Byzantium* and
Byzantium. The imaginative worlds created by J.R.R. Tolkien are
modern mythological writings – *The Hobbit*, *The Lord of the Rings*,
The Silmarillion.

Myth in the Bible

In general, mythologies are set in the time of creation to
explain how the world is set up as it is; they can also be built up
around central historical events which were seen to determine
the shape and direction of a particular people or nation. A myth
is serious business. It can be described as a symbolic story or
complex of stories that suggest or evoke a truth. It can contain
elements of fact mixed in with fantasy. In some way, men and
women have seen in many of their myths a way of
understanding the inner meaning of life and the origins of the
universe and a way of engaging themselves in that meaning.
The myths also have a role in maintaining the stability of the
present state. They give them a purpose and direction because,
according to the story myths of creation, all that exists is rooted
in decision; they are planned events rather than passing fluid
chance.

Very often, the proclamation of a myth was incorporated
into ritual. They express themselves there in symbolic activities,
dance, drama, and rites. The combination of word and ritual
together facilitates the believers' integration into their universe
and relationships.

Right across the world in many cultures there are stories
about the origins of the universe and the creation of the human
race. Genesis takes and remodels fragments of creation
mythologies that were common in the Middle Eastern culture
of the time. One of these is Enuma Elish[7], a text that dates back
to the early part of the second millennium BCE. It describes the

creation of the universe. In the beginning were the waters. The
gods themselves emerged from the waters. There follows a
time of battle and chaos among the gods. Evil was overcome
and from it came the creation of the human person. The
meaning of human existence is to contain that evil and serve
the gods. 'Thus the guilt which had come into being in the
divine realm is enclosed and externalised in the mortal
existence of man, prey to all kind of evil. At the same time, the
gods themselves are freed from it. Men serve the gods through
the cult. But as a preliminary to this, they already serve the gods
through their very existence – since they are basically nothing
more that the evil rejected from the divine realm, which
thereby becomes pure and holy again. The consequences of
this mythological statement for a theology of evil are clear. Evil
is involved in the very existence of man. It has come to him
from the divine realm itself. The meaning of human existence
lies in the inclusion of evil in his life'.[8]

The Epic of Gilgamesh also dates to the early part of the
second millennium BCE. Gilgamesh is seared and shocked by
the death of his friend and this also will be his fate. He goes in
search of the plant of immortality. To escape a flood he builds
a boat taking with him on board 'the seed of all living things'.
When the boat comes to rest on a mountain he sends out
various birds, a dove, a swallow, a raven. Then he offers
sacrifices for his delivery. He finds the plant of immortality at
the bottom of the sea but it is stolen by a snake.

The Genesis mythology has points of contact but springs
from a totally different vision. Creation is good, 'God saw that
it was good', and evil entered into human life by choice and not
chance. '... the content and the orientation of mythical thought
have been profoundly modified by the historic faith of Israel'.[9]

Epic in the Bible
The religious memories of Judaism and the Christian faith are
nourished by the great epics of their tradition, that expressed

the interplay between divine action and human response. There was the call of Abraham from his country, family and his father's house to become the father of a new nation, Gen 12:1, and his journeys to Egypt. In Egypt the Lord heard the cry of a weak and oppressed people. 'By his strong arm and outstretched hand' he liberated them. 'You yourselves have seen what I did with the Egyptians, how I carried you on eagle's wings and brought you to myself', Ex 19:4. The crossing of the Red Sea, the years of travel in the wilderness of Sinai, the Covenant and the conquest of the land have rooted the faith in place, time and relationship. These epics have situated our belief in the warp and woof of history. The Bible carried on the stamp of that character. The purposes of God were seen in the rise of the David dynasty. 'He became greater and greater for the Lord, the God of hosts, was with him' 2 Sam 5:10. The invasions, disasters, exiles visited on this people were directed by God in the unfolding of his plan. The Assyrian was 'the rod of his anger', Is 10:5. Nebuchadnezzor, king of Babylon, was his 'servant', Jer 27:6 and Cyrus who liberated them was his 'anointed', Is 45:1. The prophets hammered home the central role of relationship in religious experience: justice, fair play, concern for the weak and defenceless. 'Anyone who opens a prophetic book stumbles on passionate social criticism on almost every page'.[10] There is a clear sense that the zone of 'sacred time' is the community of human beings, and that human behaviour has implications well beyond the present. Magic, destiny, blind imponderable forces have receded completely into the background. It is in the course of human events that God's struggle to implant his kingdom takes place.

Then, a new phase, a new time begins with the historical life of Jesus of Nazareth, 'the time has come', Mk 1:14. This is followed by the epic journeys of Paul and the struggles of the little Christian communities to establish themselves in the world. In all of this, word and deed, epic and revelation are intertwined in human life. According to the Second Vatican

Council, 'This economy of Revelation is realised by deeds and words, which are intrinsically bound up with each other. As a result, the works performed by God in the history of salvation show forth and bear out the doctrine and realities signified by the words; the words, for their part, proclaim the works, and bring to light the mystery they contain'.[11]

Apocalyptic texts in the Bible

Another literary style is apocalyptic. Elements of it are found in many parts of the Bible. Most of the book of Daniel is in this genre, as is the book of Revelations itself and several of the sermons of Christ. This is a literary form that is full of images and mystery. 'I saw a beast emerge from the sea: it had seven heads and ten horns, with a coronet on each of its ten horns, and its heads were marked with blasphemous titles', Rev 13:1. 'Immediately after the distress of those days the sun will be darkened, the moon will lose its brightness, the stars will fall from the sky and the powers of heaven will be shaken', Mt 24:29. There can be a bewildering kaleidoscope of images and scenes, great earthquakes and signs in the heavens, the moon becoming blood red and stars falling from their place. The immediate impression created by this sort of literature is its strangeness. Certainly, over the centuries, the striking and often disturbing imagery of the apocalyptic literature has been analysed and interpreted. Indeed, the word 'apocalyptic' is popularly associated with fanatical millenarian expectation. Texts from this literature are used to discern times, dates, and events.

Very often attempts are made to isolate the exact meaning of the images used. However, in the process, the point of apocalypse is lost. Apocalypse is a mood literature directed as much to feelings as insight and, to generate this mood, the images pile up in a rich tapestry of colour. The mindset of apocalyptic piety would dwell on the intervention of God to dispose of this corrupt world and introduce a kingdom of light and goodness. In every age, men and women are presented with the universal, intractable problems of life. Why should the innocent suffer? Is there any hope for one's personal and communal history? Why should the wicked triumph? These are perennial and unfathomable problems. The imagery of apocalyptic gives a sense of a doom-laden present but also an overwhelming impression of the power of God who draws all things to a triumphant conclusion. In spite of present suffering, God will intervene to destroy evil and bring to birth a new heaven and a new earth. The aim of this type of writing was to encourage and strengthen the faith of those who remained faithful even as they were shaken by fear and insecurity.

The Book of Revelations, the last book of the Bible, is an example of apocalyptic literature. The community is under threat from various sources. As seen by the author, one of the greatest threats was that posed by social and economic issues that could lead to Christian self-destruction. The author warns against the dissipation of value and principle. In colourful phraseology this is the message of the first four chapters. There is the terror of persecution, the fear and discomfort of the prison cell, there are the memories of friends, neighbours, family members who suffered torture and death. The suffering of the just is the basic theme of the rest of the book. The four horses evoke invasion, war, famine and death, Rev 6. There are further chapters describing triumph and destruction. Babylon becomes the code name for the Roman Empire and its evil and fall are described in Rev 17-18. Throughout the book, the forces of destruction and the forces of creation battle one another for victory. The theme of triumph comes to the fore as the book ends in a magnificent description of the future. It is a finale full of imagery and power, as the forces of creation win out. There is victory, a new heaven and a new earth, Rev 21-22:5.

4

Biblical Texts

4.1   THE HEBREW SCRIPTURES

Exodus 20:1-21 The Ten Commandments

The Hebrew Law
The Law was seen as the cherished possession of the People of God. The psalms sing of the Law being continually in the mind of the faithful, to be meditated night and day, a privileged gift. The Law is far more than a collection of legal texts. Central to the Law is the idea of Covenant. The word covenant is another word for agreement, pact, and treaty. The covenant on Mount Sinai was seen as a contract made between God and his people. It assured stability in their relationship with God, a lucid picture of the divine will and promise, and a clear understanding of the way of life God expected of the Israelites.

    The Book of Deuteronomy is strong on the idea of electing, divine love as the force behind the covenant. It was no goodness or qualities within the People that led God to give them this gift; it was just his love, Deut 7:7. The covenant was inaugurated out of the compassion of God for an enslaved people. Its continuance depends on the constancy of character of this God who had chosen them; there is constant reference to the steadfast love and faithfulness of God, cf. Ex 34:6f. He committed himself to that rescuing care and they in turn committed themselves to the way of life revealed to them by God. The various laws and regulations associated with the divine appearances in the Exodus tradition are attempts to spell out for Israel the implications of this covenant relationship. The Law is the way in which the People is meant to walk if it is to walk hand in hand with God.

The Ten Commandments

In general, the laws spell out the implications of the treaty-covenant. At the heart or core of the legal system is the Decalogue. In the Hebrew tradition, they are described as the ten words, Deut 4:13, coming directly from God and written by him on the tablets of stone, Ex 31:18; Deut 4:13; 9:9.

It is important to remember, however, that even though the Ten Commandments are an important directive on the way we should live in the presence of God, they are not an exhaustive expression of Old Testament morality. The Old Testament teaches a rich social ethic around the sharing of wealth and the treatment of the weaker members of society, Lev 19:9-17; Jer 7:6, that is not found explicitly in the Decalogue.

The Decalogue is found in two versions: Ex 20:2-17. and Deut 5:6-10, and both are perhaps expressions of an original shorter edition.

The *first* commandment, Exod 20:3, is a demand for an exclusive loyalty. In a world of many pantheons and families of God, Yahweh stands alone as the God of this particular people. This is the first step of a long process towards strict monotheism, Is 45:5.

The *second* commandment, Exod 20:4 is on imageless worship. At that time, the gods and goddesses were represented in many forms – human, animal, fish – but there is to be no representation of Yahweh. An image is something produced by human energy and imagination. It is limited, static. Having power over the image, human hands place it in a certain spot and can move it at will. In other words, making an image is seen as an attempt to define God according to human categories and in the end to control him. This conflicts with the free, majestic and often demanding God that is portrayed in the Bible. The only witness or image of God that is allowed is God's own word.

The taking of God's name in vain, Exod 20:7, refers to the misuse of God's name. The abuse of God's name in the sin of perjury might be the primary issue here. 'You shall not swear by my name falsely,' Lev 19:12. There could also be an evil use of the divine name in which God is invoked to cause harm. Frivolous, disrespectful use of the divine name is also prohibited.

The *fourth* commandment, Exod 20:8, is on Sabbath work. This underlines both God's claim on a proportion of our time and energy and the dignity of the human person. On the latter point, it blocks any attempt to define human life in terms of productivity and service; there is a divine approval of the role of rest and leisure. According to the Exodus version of this commandment, observing the Sabbath is entering into the rest of God after the six days of creation. It is a time of joyful contented contemplation of the wonders of life. Deuteronomy links it with the freedom from captivity in Egypt, Deut 5:15. As slaves there, they were defined in terms of feverish productivity.

The *last six* demands are on human relationships within the covenant community, Exod 20:12-17. A link between religion and social and personal morality is not found in all beliefs. If we take this for granted, it is only because we stand within a Judaeo-Christian heritage that stems from the Decalogue.

The first commandment in this section is addressed to adults whose parents are elderly, Exod 20:12. Their energy and vitality may be spent, but respect is still their due. Without this, the stability of family life is undermined. Honour for those who have given life ensures a good life for those who received it.

Capital punishment or pacifism is not an issue in the *sixth* commandment, Exod 20:13. It is more a question of not taking the law into one's own hands. The normal channels of justice in society are to be used.

The *seventh* commandment, Exod 20:14, acknowledges the betrayal and anguish caused by infidelity. As God's love can make exclusive demands, so too does its image in the affection and care that man and wife have for each other.

Every society prohibits the theft of property and this is catered for in the *eighth* commandment, Exod 20:15.

The *ninth* commandment, Exod 20:16, defends a person's right to a fair trial; no legal system can operate if people are able to get away with lying in court.

The *final* commandment, Exod 20:17, deepens the attitude of respect for others' property by introducing the idea of covetousness. The Hebrew word for 'covet' means the whole process involved in thievery. This begins with the entertaining of the idea of theft, conspiracy, the planning and execution of the act.

The Dutch Catechism explores commandments in this fashion: 'We offer a preliminary consideration of the word 'commandment'. Many understand this as a burden imposed upon man from outside. They imagine that they would behave quite differently if there were no commandments. But this way of thinking debases the commandments to something that would be concerned with matters of no value in themselves. Honesty, reverence for life, material fidelity, respect for others, would not be valuable in themselves, but merely precepts imposed by a God who could have chosen others. Such attitudes are often the result of an education where the good is too strongly emphasised as a system of well-defined precepts; of a general atmosphere where too much stress is laid on the extrinsic 'must' and too little confidence placed in the intrinsic and spontaneous sense of values in both pupils and educators. The result is that the truth that the commandments are good in themselves is lost sight of. We people forget that they are in themselves most profound and vital values, which are already anchored in the nature of man and of the world'.[1]

1 Sam. 2:1-10 Hannah's Song of Thanks

The Context

Hannah lived roughly around the year 1050 BCE. It was a time when the Jewish settlements occupied the spiny, mountainous ridge that ran the length of the country. The Jewish villages were organised in clans or tribes. They had no real political cohesion. On occasion, in times of crisis, a tribe was led by a leader whom they called a Judge. Dotted in these areas were Canaanite cities with agricultural hinterlands. The Philistines inhabited the coastlands. Then to the East lay vast waste tracts of desert.

The song emerges from the context of national and personal oppression. The Jewish people are under pressure from the Philistines. Hannah, herself, is childless. She is one of the two wives of Elkanah. The other wife, Peninnah, has had children and uses the fact to demean Hannah. The sacred shrine, the Tent of Meeting, or the Tabernacle of ancient Israel was kept in Shiloh, Jos 18:1. The Ark of the Covenant, which contained the tablets given to Moses, Exod 25:10-16, was there, 1 Sam 3:3. On one of the yearly visits to the sanctuary there, Hannah prayed for a child. The priest Eli promised that her prayer would be answered. Hannah gave birth to a son and she called him Samuel. Hannah sees the birth of the child as a clear sign of God's regard for her. If she has received the child as a gift, she is bound to return it as a gift again. When the child was weaned, she brought him to Shiloh where she dedicated him to the service of the Lord there, 1 Sam 1:28. Samuel lived in Shiloh and was visited each year by his family. Subsequently, Hannah gave birth to three sons and two daughters.

Hannah's Song

The song is a hymn of praise to God. It is full of delight and confidence. The focus is on the power of God to give security and cause change. For his people, God is the stability and strength of a foundation rock, 1 Sam.2:2. At the end of Psalm 19, God is described 'O Lord, my rock and my redeemer', Ps 19:14. God's measured knowledge cuts through all vanity and arrogance, 1 Sam 2:3. God reverses the fortunes of the poor and the powerful, 1 Sam 2:4-5. God has the power to give life or withhold it, 1 Sam 2:6. In Israelite understanding, Sheol is a place of darkness, weakness and distress. God's special concern for the poor and helpless is a feature of the Biblical tradition. In the prophets, this is a much emphasised theme, Amos 2:6; 5:11; Is.1:17, 23; 3:14-15. The horizons of the song widen in v.8. God is in control of all creation. In one Israelite understanding of the world, it is seen as mounted on pillars. 'When the earth totters, and all its inhabitants, it is I who keep steady its pillars', Ps 75:3. In this new context, the faithful are protected and the wicked fail, v.9. God, the universal judge, gives strength to the king whose role is to mediate justice, Is 11:1-9.

There was no king in Israel in Hannah's time. The reference to the monarchy seems to indicate that the song was composed at a much later period and put into the lips of Hannah. However, the king reference is appropriate here because it will be Hannah's son, Samuel, who will anoint the first king, 1 Sam 10:1. The arrival of Samuel marks the beginning of a momentous chain of events that will completely change the history of the people. There will be a king. Shiloh itself will fade from the scene, and Jerusalem will become the new religious and political capital of the nation. Consequently, the psalm puts the birth and subsequent career of Samuel among the great acts of God.

Hannah's God

In the song, God is seen as one actively involved in the human struggle. This is a typically Biblical understanding of God. He is always described in relationship to his people; he is seen in his willingness to be with people. God is known as one who chose the people to be his very own, delivering them from slavery, fashioning a nation out of a motley rabble and giving them his law and promise. 'I have seen the affliction of my people ... I know their sufferings, and I have come down to deliver them', Ex 3:7-8.

Hannah's Song and the Magnificat
There is an obvious resemblance between this text in Samuel and Mary's hymn, the Magnificat in Luke 1:46-58. In both cases, two women delight in the divine intervention that led to the birth of their child. As in Samuel's birth, the birth of Jesus also marks a new beginning, with the promise of a revolutionary change reversing the fortunes of the rich and poor.

Isaiah 52:13-53:12 Israel restored

The Book of Isaiah
The book of Isaiah is an anthology of material coming from a period which spans over two hundred years. The first thirty-nine chapters are the words of Isaiah son of Amoz, whose prophetic activity continued in Jerusalem from the seven hundred and forties BCE to the end of the century. Chapters forty to fifty-five are the oracles of an anonymous prophet usually called Second-Isaiah or Deutero-Isaiah who was a member of the Jewish community living in Babylon about 540 BCE. His name is unknown, but he was a man of great genius who met the dejection of the exiles with a message of hope in a New Age that God was about to bring about. Finally, chapters fifty-six to sixty-six contain a large number of miscellaneous passages reflecting conditions in Palestine some time after the rebuilding of the Temple in 516 BCE.

The unit, Isaiah 52:13-53:12 is from the block of material called Second Isaiah. It was written in exile in Babylon and dates from around 540 BCE.

The Servant Songs

It is customary to isolate four oracles in the Book and call them the Servant Songs, Is 42:1-4; 49:1-6; 50:4-9; 52:13-53:12. The names come from a central mysterious person who features in these texts and is called 'the Servant'.

Who then is this servant? Is he an individual, or is he a group within the People of God? Does he stand for all Israel? This is an ancient problem. In the New Testament, we read of the Ethiopian finance minister who on his way home from Jerusalem was puzzled about this very point, Acts 8:26ff. There is still no great agreement. Writing about the author of Second Isaiah, Klaus Koch wonders, 'Did he envisage the death of an individual, through which the sins of other people would be forgiven? Or is the Jewish interpretation right, when it sees here the path of suffering trodden by the Jewish people?'.[2]

There is no need to have exclusive theories on the issue. According to Oscar Cullman, biblical salvation history unfolds from beginning to end according to the principle of representation in a progressive reduction.[3] The Bible opens with the vision of all creation and then proceeds from the whole creation to humanity as representing creation, then from humanity to the people of Israel as representing humanity, from the people of Israel to the 'remnant' as standing for Israel and finally from the remnant to a single, man Jesus. Like the Hebrew idea of the king, the servant is one and the same time an individual personality and the whole or part of the people of Israel. Sometimes, he can be spoken of in terms of the one and other times in terms of the many. There are multiple layers of meaning in the text. On one level, it can include the expiatory suffering of a mysterious individual; on another, the sufferings of the people in exile on behalf of the wider Israelite community; and, finally indeed, the pain of all innocent peoples who died through the violence of others.

Perhaps the immediate objective of Second Isaiah was to make sense of the sufferings of those brought into exile in Babylon. With him in exile were old people who had been devout from their youth. They still lived with the memory of seeing their family and friends butchered in Jerusalem by the Babylonians. They could recall their friends and relatives collapsing to the ground from exhaustion, famine and sickness during the frightful journey to Babylon. Then, there were faithful young people born in Exile who had no part in the foolishness that brought ruin to Jerusalem. Why should they suffer and why should so many people live in the border of despair?

The Restoration of Israel and the Meaning of its Suffering

In the fourth servant song, which contains some of the best known passages in the Old Testament, the author deals with restoration and suffering.

He begins in a note of hope. The crushed and captive Israel will be restored, Is 52:13-15. This hopeful message is contrary to human expectations and this change of fortunes will amaze the nations and the kings, Is 52:15.

Having proclaimed a message of confidence and hope, the author now develops the theme of suffering. This affliction will be endured on behalf of others. The community reflects on the whole thing. It is not said who 'we', Is 53:1, are. It is either Israel in exile, or Israel in general now reflecting on itself and its history. The mysterious person grew up utterly insignificant, 'a young plant and like a root out of dry ground', v.2. His suffering was not just an incident; it was an ongoing process, v.2-3. A confession now interrupts the report, v.4. They believed that he was suffering because of his own faults and so smitten by God. They see now that he was a vicarious sufferer. He bore the sins of others and the punishment which results from them, v.5. His annihilation was complete. He suffered, v.7; died, v.8, and was buried v.9. The Servant's suffering involved shame. It did not end with his death. He was buried with the wicked, v.9. It is clear from this verse that the Servant was an individual and that he actually died and was buried.

The Servant is in his grave but the account goes on to say that he will prosper, v.10. This prosperity is described in the traditional language of offspring and long life. Through the servant, God will justify others, 11b-12.

The final verse 12 gives a summary of the mission of the servant: to bear their iniquities, he poured out his soul, he was numbered with the transgressors, he bore the sin of many, and he made intercession for the transgressors.

Many attempts have been made to identify the Servant of this passage. Is it Israel? Is it the author of Second Isaiah himself? Is it some other biblical character or an unknown individual? No identification is satisfactory, but there is no doubt about the New Testament understanding of the Servant in Is 52:13-53:12. He is Christ.

The Servant in the New Testament
These texts were a rich mine for New Testament theologians. When Jesus is called the chosen one at the baptism in Mk 1:11, it seems to allude to Is 42:1. Matthew quotes the whole of the first servant song, Is 42:1-4, in the context of Jesus' ministry, Mt 12:15-21. Jesus is described as 'the Lamb of God who takes away the sins of the world', Jn 1:29; cf. Is 53:7, 12. Jesus is described as coming 'to give his life as a ransom for many' in Mk 10:45. This understanding of Christ's role has its roots in Is 53:10-12. Jesus applies to himself the words from Is 53:9, 'he was reckoned with the transgressors' in Lk 22.37. The theme of Israel's destiny to be 'light to the nations', Is 42:6;49:6, is taken up by Simeon in the Temple, Lk 2:32. In the Acts of the Apostles, Acts 8:26-35, the deacon Philip interprets Is 53:7-8 in terms of Jesus.

4.2   THE NEW TESTAMENT

Mark 9:2-13 The Transfiguration

The general context of this account is of particular interest. There is a central unit in the Gospel of Mark, 8:22-10:52. This is framed by healings of blind men, 8:22-26 and 10:46-52. The healing of the blind man at Bethsaida, 8:22-26, seems to run in tandem with the healing of the blind Bartimaeus, which is narrated in 10:45-52. In between, the curtain comes up on the first details of Jesus' own personal passion and the difficulty, if not the impossibility, of the disciples to grasp this. The two healings evoke the struggle of Jesus to open the eyes of his disciples to the truth of suffering in their and his experience. 'What Jesus does on behalf of the two blind men at the beginning and at the end, he tries to do on behalf of the disciples all the way through'.[4] However, the disciples seem to be quite incapable of grasping what Jesus is teaching them.

Those disciples who were with Jesus in other critical moments, Mk 5:37; 14:33, now get a glimpse into whom he is and the final result of his mission. Some commentators would hold that this is a resurrection appearance transferred back to the public ministry. However, one of the few chronological indications found in the Gospel link it with the Caesarea Philippi confession: 'after six days'. In the mind of Mark, it is firmly rooted in the time before the death and resurrection. Even the change in Luke, from six to 'about eight days', Lk 9:28, underlines the link with a definite time and place.

In a tradition going back to the early fourth century, the Transfiguration has been located on Mount Tabor that rises to a height of 1850 feet. However, the mountain is not named in any of the Gospel texts.

In the appearances of the two men, v.4, Jesus is integrated into the wellsprings of Judaic tradition, the Law represented by Moses, and the Prophets in the person of Elijah. He is the one for whom they are about! The reference to the three huts in v.5 seems to reflect Peter's desire to perpetuate the experience. It was not to be, because the disciples must return to the lowlands of suffering. The cloud which envelops them in v.7 is a traditional image of the divine presence, Exod 16:10; 19:9; 24:15-16; 33:9. It gathers in the disciples too, introducing them to this presence, and the voice from heaven says to the three and to all Mark's readers, 'Listen to him'. In Mark's Gospel specific attention would be drawn to the teaching that suffering is the path to glory, 8:31; 9:12; 10:34. The doctrine has the divine approval.

Jesus' importance is emphasised by the departure of Moses and Elijah. The tradition and teaching authority now flows into him and from him.

Coming down from the mountain, the main theme receives further emphasis, v.9. Glory, resurrection are forged in the fires of suffering. Continuing along these lines, in vs.11-13, there is a discussion on the coming of Elijah. If Elijah is to come, it is not in the tremendous vision that they have just seen, but rather in the hard toil, suffering and death of John the Baptist.

He has been confessed as Messiah; he has stated he must suffer. What it all leads to ultimately appears in this momentary flash of resurrection glory. This mountain insight into Jesus' true character is put in at the end of a very careful sequence. The author's general teaching is that there is no life without death – no Easter without a crucifixion. So this glimpse into the real identity of Jesus is given only after words of suffering.

The account in its setting illustrates profound realities in the human experience. We cannot keep going without some dream or glimpse of light at the end of the tunnel. When that light comes, the tents will be built and last forever. Neither can we deny or run from the brutal reality which life often is.

Luke 6:20-49 The Sermon on the Mount

The Social Gospel of Luke
The Sermon on the Mount in Luke is introduced by the establishment of the Christian community. Jesus spends the

night in prayer on the mountain, 6:12. He descends from the heights to take decisive action. Jesus calls the Twelve whom he named apostles, 6:12-16. They are the nucleus of the New Israel, the New People of God. As the old People of God were descended from twelve individuals, the twelve sons of Jacob, Gen 35:22-26, so too will the new.

Luke then proceeds to outline the values of this new community. Like every other passage, Luke's presentation of the Sermon on the Mount fits into a general context and reflects attitudes that are embodied in the whole Gospel. Christ in Luke is the friend of the poor, the sick, and the women, all of whom were downgraded and repressed. The beatitudes and woes teach that the roles of the rich and the poor will be reversed, 6:20-26. This is also a theme in the Magnificat, Lk 1:52-53. God is the one who 'puts down the proud and raises the lowly', Lk 1:52. Accordingly, Jesus himself is born in a stable, Lk 2:7. Impressive Eastern wise men do not welcome him into the world but the totally uneducated shepherds in the fields, Lk 2:16. Two very ordinary people receive him in the temple, Lk 2:25,36. In the parable of the rich man and Lazarus, Lk 16:19-31, the rich man is condemned because he was content to accept a social situation in which he feasted and was well off while Lazarus starved. Only in Luke do we get the social message of John the Baptist to the multitudes, the tax-collectors, and the soldiers, 3:10-14. In 11:40-41, Jesus attacks the Pharisees. They measure ritual purification by impersonal actions. Almsgiving is what really purifies. 'But give for alms those things which are within: and behold, everything is clean for you', 11:41. The gift must also express inner attitudes of mercy and care and flow from the heart. Only Luke tells the story of Zacchaeus in chapter 19:1-10. He seeks out Christ; receives him joyfully; he gives to the needy and restores to those whom he had defrauded, 'so today salvation has come to this home', 19:9. The sharing of possessions is a characteristic of the idealised community in Jerusalem. 'And all who believed were together and had all things in common; and they sold their possessions and goods and distributed them to all, as any had need', Acts 2:44-45 and 4:32-34. It is useful to remember that the giving of alms was not really part of the Gentile culture. It was a Jewish practice which was unknown in the Gentile world.

The beatitudes and curses, Lk 6:20-26

Unlike Matthew, where the beatitudes are presented as general principles, here they are addressed directly to the disciples, the new community. Although the crowd is around him, 6:17, Jesus speaks directly to his Church, 6:20. 'Blessed are you'; and 'Woe to you'. The issues come from the grind of day-to-day existence and the problems that emerge: poverty, hunger, grief and social exclusion. The beatitudes and woes continue Luke's pattern of reversal of situations. Those who are mighty are cast down; the lowly are lifted up. Each beatitude is contrasted with a woe, the poor versus the rich, the hungry and the well fed, those who weep and those who laugh, those who are acclaimed and those who are persecuted. The objective of Luke is not to contrast Christians with those outside the community but rather the social contrasts within the Church itself.

There is no blessing of poverty as such; likewise there is no blanket condemnation of riches. Poverty is an evil that is to be stamped out. When Jesus says, 'Blessed are the poor', it is not precisely because of their poverty that they are blessed. It is because of their helplessness and oppression, and so they are the subjects of God's special care and love. The poor are blessed because God is merciful, not because they are poor. Likewise, possessions are not evil in themselves. Evil arises when we turn them into gods and measure our success and worth by them. To illustrate the futility of wrapping our hearts around possession, Luke later tells a parable on the subject, the story of the rich fool, Lk 12:13-21. His foolishness arises from his belief that he has no need of God. 'So it is when a man stores up treasure for himself in place of making himself rich in the sight of God', Lk 12:21.

Radical Loving 6:27-35

The sermon proceeds to dealing with a far-reaching loving: to love one's enemies, to reject retaliation, to live with compassion and generosity, 6:27-35.

The ultimate measuring rod for our relationships with one another is the way God treats us, Lk 6:36. If that is the way, love must be extended to those who do not love you. Mutual regard, gentleness, sensitivity, justice in relationships are also the pattern of God's dealings with us. Only Luke tells the story of the totally surprising love of the father for his prodigal son, Lk 15:11-32. In his acts of generosity, God does not distinguish between the good and the evil, Lk 6:35. It is only in acting as God does that we can truly be described his sons, Lk 6:35.

Mercy and Forgiveness 6:36-42

The sayings on mercy continue what is said about love. It is an aspect of God's life that is reflected in the believer, 6:36. The character of God is such that he welcomes the despairing, hopeless sinners and rejects the self-righteous. Luke tells the story of the two standing in the temple to pray. However, it is the publican and not the Pharisee who experiences mercy, Lk 18:9-14. When we learn about ourselves, our strengths and our weakness, then we will have the knowledge to be teachers. Because of our awareness we can really see, 6:39-40. There is a real touch of humour in the hopeless exaggeration in the story of the log and the speck, 6:39-42.

The Whole Person 6:43-49

There must be a unity between what one says and does with one's heart. The sermon concludes that it is not sufficient to just call on the Lord in words. His lordship over the believer must cover the totality of the believer's life and be translated into the personal and social dimensions of his life. When a life is not integrated from foundations to roof, it will be destroyed in the first storm, Lk 6:47-9.

John 1:1-18 The Prologue

Prologues and the Gospels
All four Gospels begin with a prologue. Using the preaching of John the Baptist, Mark embodies Jesus in the prophetic dreams and aspirations of the People of God. In the genealogy, Matthew integrates Jesus in a history going back to Abraham. Luke's genealogy situates Jesus in the human race; ultimately what God is doing is to create a new humanity of which Christ is the New Adam. The Fourth Gospel, in the Prologue, goes to the limits of the created order and beyond it, to the timeless presence of God, to the time before time.

The Revelation of Love
The first chapter of the Fourth Gospel describes Jesus using terminology which was already traditional in early Christianity. Jesus is the Son of God, Jn 1:49; he is the Messiah, Jn 1:41; he is the King of Israel, Jn 1:49; he is the Lamb of God, Jn 1:29; he is the Son of Man, Jn 1:51; he is a teacher, Jn 1:38; he is the one about whom Moses and the prophets wrote, Jn 1:45.

However, Jesus as Word is the distinctive feature of the Fourth Gospel's witness. The central theme of the Prologue is revelation. Indeed, unambiguous commitment to revelation is at the heart the author's thinking. This is a revelation that focuses on the presence of eternal love manifested in the Passion. The freeing experience of salvation is precisely the experience of being totally loved, 13:34-5; 15:12-14. This love liberates in allowing one to love in turn: being able to love is the greatest form of freedom. The Fourth Evangelist is trying to convey the idea that the universe is, at its deepest level, friendly and loving and therefore liberates people to be friendly, peaceful and loving themselves, Jn 17:11,21.

'Christianity is not first of all a social message of a struggle for justice; it is not first of all "doing good to the poor"; it is an experience of God, an experience of love which is a free gift and brings us to inner freedom. This gift transforms us, liberates us from fear, and from guilt and from sin, it makes us children of the Father and friends, brothers and sisters of Jesus. Prayer is receiving in one's heart the heart of Jesus: Jesus teaching us how he loves the Father and how he loves every person, particularly the littlest and the weakest.'[5]

The endless discussions in John on the transcendent nature of Jesus stem from this issue. It is important that it is really God who is being displayed here and being experienced in the bravery, care and love of Jesus. This deep reality is also experienced as an energy that reaches towards us to transform and 'de-kink' us. This energy is described in terms of the Holy Spirit. So reality at its deepest is friendly, embracing, transforming, and healing.

The intuition of people of many traditions and many religions has reached similar conclusions. Mystics have had moments when appearances parted their veils and they got a sense of the ocean of love, a friendly benevolent spirit at the deepest level and that experience changed their lives.

In the Beginning

The Gospel starts with a statement of revelation coming out of eternity: 'In the beginning was the Word ... all things through him became.' There is a Word who was there before creation, who was God's instrument in creation. Where is that word now? The Gospel spells out the answer. The Word is in Jesus of Nazareth. Much reflection has been done on the background of this term. In the Jewish tradition, the Word of God has a power of its own which overcomes the prophet and leaves him no opportunity to suppress it, Amos 3:8; Jer 20:29; Is 55:11. In the

Wisdom literature, Wisdom is personified, Wis 7:22. After a lifetime of thought, the evangelist came to see that both Word and Wisdom come together in Jesus Christ. If these terms are personified in the Old Testament, it is because they really came to earth and lived a lifetime with men and women in Jesus Christ. 'In the beginning was the Word ... all things through him became.' Here we have contrasted: A happening, an event, a beginning, creation: something which took place at a specific moment, with the continuous existence of the Word. We are not just told that at the beginning he happened to be there, but at that moment of beginning, of start from nothingness to existence, he was in a state of continual being, he was being. The Greek tense is 'imperfect'.

It is noted that the Word was 'with the God', v. 1. This points forward to the Son 'in the bosom of the Father', v.18, which ends the Prologue. There is a technique of Hebrew composition called 'inclusion', the first and last themes echo and repeat each other.

The early prayers and hymns in the New Testament speak of the pre-existent Christ, Phil 2:6- and Col 1:15-; St Paul is on the same line in 1 Cor. 8:6; cf. also Heb 1:2ff.

Word and World

The repeated emphasis on the presence of the Word in all creation, v.3, means that existence itself is revelatory. The experience of living: relationships, pain and joy, beauty, nature are the media of the Word's message. God is within his creation and the Word lights up the inwardness of all that is and shows reality. Teilhard de Chardin puts it well, 'By means of all created things the divine assails us, penetrates us and moulds us. We imagined it as distant and inaccessible, whereas we lived steeped in its burning layers. *"In eo vivimus"*, as Jacob said awakening from his dream. The world, this palpable world which we are wont to treat with boredom and disrespect, with which we habitually regard places with no sacred association for us, is in truth a holy place and we did not know it'.[6]

Earth's crammed with heaven,
And every common bush afire with God:
But only he who sees, takes off his shoes,
The rest sit around it, and pluck blackberries.[7]

The Word is the bearer of life, v.4. Throughout the Gospel, this
is his reason for coming. He comes that we may have life and
have it to the full, that his joy may be our joy and that our joy
may be complete. Basically this life is union with him and Jesus
speaks of it at the last supper under the image of the vine and
the branches, Jn 15:1-11.

In Genesis 1, which is clearly evoked in these verses, God
said: 'let there be light', v.3. In the context of chaos,
shapelessness, stormy waters, raging winds, with light came
the emergence of clarity, form and meaning in the universe.
John pursues the theme of light and darkness, v. 4-5, but in the
context of human affairs, moral conduct, and the direction of
life. The moral chaos and darkness through which we must
chart a course is caught vividly by the poet Matthew Arnold
and the Italian Jewish concentration camp survivor, Primo
Levi:

And we are here as on a darkling plain
Swept with confused alarms of struggle and flight,
Where ignorant armies clash by night.[8]

... we too are so dazzled by power and prestige as to
forget our essential fragility: willingly or not we come to
terms with power, forgetting that we are all in the ghetto,
that the ghetto is walled in, that outside the ghetto reign
the lords of death and that close by the train is waiting.[9]

In vs.6-8, John the Baptist witnesses to the role of the Word as
light.

The world of v.9 is the universe of men and women. It is the world that God loves and tries to save. 'God so loved the world', 3:16; 'He gives life to the world', 4:42. Christ has come not to 'condemn the world but to save it', 12:47.

Word and Israel

The whisper of revelation in creation becomes more audible in the experience of the People of God. He comes in the choice of Israel as God's special people, 'to his own people', v.11. The roots of this idea are found in the Wisdom themes of the Old Testament. 'Over waters of the sea, over all the land, over every people and nation I held sway. Among all these I sought a resting place; in whose inheritance should I abide? Then the Creator of all gave me his command, and he who formed me chose the spot for my tent, saying, "In Jacob made your dwelling, in Israel your inheritance"', Sirach 24:6-8. See Jn 8; 1 Cor 10:4.

The rebirth of those who received the Word in Old Testament times does not depend on race, blood or soil, but on a divine initiative meeting a response of love and faith, v.13.

Word and Incarnation

The climax of revelation comes with the incarnation of the Word in Jesus Christ, v.14. This verse is loaded with meaning. There is reference again to Word. This Word became flesh; it did not just take flesh but identified itself with flesh. 'Here we have an explicit statement of incarnation, the first, and indeed only such statement in the NT'.[10] The word 'flesh' refers to the sphere of the human, the worldly as opposed to the divine; 'what is born of the flesh is flesh, what is born of the spirit is spirit', 3:6; 'it is the spirit that gives life, the flesh has nothing to offer', 6:63; 'you judge according to the flesh, I judge noone', 8:15. The flesh therefore is not just another neutral word for saying 'human'; it is becoming a human person in all its transitoriness, helplessness and vanity, Is 40:6; Rom 8:3. The

Word 'dwelt among us'. A literal translation from the Greek would read, 'the Word tabernacled among us'. The flesh of Christ is the new localisation of the divine presence on earth and the replacement of ancient tabernacles, Jn 2:19-22, Rev 21:22: 'I saw no temple in the city. The Lord, God the Almighty, is its temple – he and the Lamb'. The phrase 'full of grace and truth' is redolent of Old Testament associations. The grace of God is his kindness; and his truth is his truthfulness to himself and his promises; he is loyal to his covenant. 'The Lord, a God merciful and gracious, slow to anger and abounding in steadfast love and faithfulness', Exod 34:6. When the evangelist uses the term 'we saw', he means the quality of sight/faith of those who were involved with Jesus during the period of his earthly ministry, Jn 20:22; 1 Jn 1:1ff. It is more than physical vision but it includes it.

> When my ashes scatter', says John, 'there is left on earth
> No one alive who knew (consider this!)
> -Saw with his eyes and handled with his hands
> That which was from the first, the Word of Life.
> How will it be when none more saith, 'I saw'?[11]

They saw his 'glory'. In the Old Testament, God's glory appears when he reveals himself dramatically as 'mighty-to-care'. As the term suggests, they got a sight of his 'wonder' and so it happened at the first miracle in Cana, Jn 2:11. However, as the Gospel progresses, glory takes on an unexpected dimension. With savage paradox, the Cross itself is the revelation of the glory of God, Jn 17:1. The wonder of God is expressed in a man pinned to the Cross. 'John ... in the picture presented in his Gospel ... bathes the outwardly insignificant and unsuccessful life of Jesus, which comes to a tragic end, in a glorious light and transforms its terrible end into a dazzling success and victory, though admittedly only for the eyes of believers. He has turned the process of cross followed by resurrection, humiliation followed by exaltation, into a single process in which apparent humiliation is already exaltation and the outward degradation of Jesus in reality his glorification'.[12] The phrase 'only begotten' makes no assertion about the nature of Jesus; he is especially beloved of the Father. Yet there is evidence that Jesus used this sonship of himself in a special sense, Jn 19:7. In Christ, all the love, all the light, all the life of God is there as love added to love, v.16.

Conclusion

No-one has ever seen God, v.18, and so life remains shrouded in uncertainty. The key to life is missing. The Son unfolds the mystery of existence. He does so as one who is at the bosom of the Father, not as an infant, but lying there as was the custom in the intimate companionship of a meal.

Notes

1   The Bible as Living Classic and Sacred Text

1. F. Kermode, *The Classic*, London: Faber and Faber, 1975, 44.
2. N. Frye, *The Great Code. Bible and Literature,* New York and London: Harcourt Brace Jovanovich, 1981, xi-xii.
3. Vatican Council II, *Dei Verbum: Dogmatic Constitution on Divine Revelation,* A. Flannery (ed.), *Vatican Collection,* vol. 1, Dublin: Dominican Publications, 1992, 756.
4. *Dei Verbum,* 11.
5. P.J. Achtemeier, *Inspiration and Authority,* Massachusetts: Hendrickson Publishers, 1999, 105.
6. B. Anderson, *The Living Word of the Bible,* London: Longmans, 1979, 17.

2   Text and Community

1. J.J. Hayes and J.M. Miller, *Israelite and Judaean History,* London: SCM, 1977, 70-142.
2. C. Westermann, *Genesis 1-11,* London: SCM, 1984, 7.
3. E.H. Carr, *What is History?,* Harmondsworth: Penguin, 1964, 23.
4. R.G. Collingwood, in Editor's Preface to *The Idea of History,* Oxford: Oxford University Press, 1961, xii.
5. G. von Rad, *Deuteronomy. The Interpreter's Dictionary of the Bible,* Vol.1, Nashville: Abingdon, 1962, 837.
6. L. Boadt, *Reading the Old Testament. An Introduction,* New York: Paulist Press, 1984, 449.
7. W. Eichrodt, *Theology of the Old Testament,* vol. 1, London: SCM, 1960, 38.
8. Pliny the Younger, *Letters to Trajan,* no. 10, 96

9. L. Grollenberg, *Jesus,* London: SCM, 1978, 2.

10. C. Osiek, *What are they saying about the social setting of the New Testament?,* New York: Paulist Press, 1984, 41.

11. J. Stambaugh and D. Balch, *The Social World of the First Christians,* London: SPCK, 1986, 53.

12. J. Stambaugh and D. Balch, op. cit., 55.

13. W. Meeks, *The First Urban Christians. The Social World of the Apostle Paul,* New Haven: Yale University Press, 1983, 74.

14. H. Felder, *Christ and the Critics,* vol. 1, London: Burns Oates and Washbourne Ltd., 1924, 116.

15. R. Bultmann, *Jesus and the Word,* London : Fontana Books, 1958, 14.

16. Patagonia Latina, 267, 354A.

17. R. Brown, K. Donfried, J. Reumann, *Peter in the New Testament,* London: Chapman, 1974, 23.

18. J. Dunn, *The Living Word,* London: SCM, 1987, 34.

19. V. Taylor, *The Formation of the Gospel Tradition,* London: SPCK, 1935, 175.

20. P. Achtemeier, *Mark,* Philadelphia: Fortress Press, 1975, 6.

21. W. Arndt and F.W. Gingrich, *A Greek-English Lexicon of the New Testament and Other Early Christian Literature,* Chicago: University of Chicago Press, 1957, 624.

22. A.J.B. Higgens, 'The Preface to Luke and the Kerygma in Acts,' in W. Gasque and R. Martin (eds), *Apostolic History and the Gospel,* Exeter: 1970, 82.

23. J.M. Creed, *The Gospel According to St Luke,* London: Macmillan, 1930, 5.

24. H.G. Kee, *Community of the New Age,* London: SCM, 1977, 30.

25. M. Dibelius, *From Tradition to Gospel*, English trans., New York: 1934, 3.

26. G. Bornkamm, 'End-Expectation and Church in Matthew' in G. Bornkamm (ed.), *Tradition and Interpretation in Matthew,* London: SCM, 1963, 15.

3   The Literature of the Bible

1. J. Shea, *Stories of Faith,* Illinois: The Thomas More Press, 1980, 89.

2. W.J. Bausch, *Storytelling. Imagination and Faith* Connecticut: Twenty-Third Publications, 1984, 21.

3. J. Jeremias, *The Parables of Jesus*, Revised Edition, London: SCM Press Ltd, 1963, 173-4.

4. S. Heaney, *Preoccupations. Selected Prose 1968–1978,* London: Faber and Faber, 1984, 48.

5. T. Kearney, 'Beyond the Planter and the Gael', Interview with John Hewitt and John Montague on Northern Poetry and the Troubles. *The Crane Bag,* vol. 4, no.2 (1980–1).

6. C. Westermann, *The Living Psalms,* Edinburgh: T. and T. Clarke, 1989, 16.

7. The texts of biblical-related mythologies are found in a volume edited by J.B. Prichard, *Ancient Near Eastern Texts Relating to the Bible,* Princeton: Princeton University Press, 1950.

8. N. Lohfink, *The Christian Meaning of the Old Testament,* London: Burns and Oates, 1969, 56.

9. A.-M. Dubarle, *Le Péché Originel dans l'Écriture,* Paris, 1958, 53, quoted in J. McKenzie, 'Myth and the Old Testament', *Myths and Realities,* London: Chapman, 1963, 197.

10. K. Koch, *The Prophets,* London: SCM, 1982, vol. 2, 190.

11. Vatican Council II, *Dogmatic Constitution on Divine Revelation*, 1-2, in A. Flannery (ed.), *Vatican Collection,* vol. 1, Dublin, 1992, 751.

4   Biblical texts

1. *A New Catechism. The Catholic Faith for Adults,* London, 1967, 371.

2. K. Koch, *The Prophets,* vol. 2, London: SCM, 1983, 140.

3. O. Cullmann, *Christ and Time,* London: SCM, 1951, 116.

4. W.H. Kelber, *Mark's Story of Jesus,* Philadelphia: Fortress, 1979, 44.

5. Jean Vanier, in his introduction to T. Philippe, *The Contemplative Life. A Theological Retreat,* London, 1990.

6. Teilhard de Chardin, *The Divine Milieu,* London: Collins, 1964, 112.

7. Elizabeth Barrett Browning, *Aurora Leigh* (1857), Book 7.

8. Matthew Arnold, *Dover Beach.*

9. P. Levi, *The Drowned and the Saved,* London: Michael Joseph, 1988, 51.

10. J. Dunn, *Christology in the Making,* 2nd edn, London: SCM, 1989, 241.

11. Robert Browning, *A Death in the Desert.*

12. R. Schnackenburg, *The Gospel According to St John,* vol. 2, London: Burns and Oates, 1980, 408.